S0-BIY-234

THE PROBLEM OF AUTHORITY
IN THE CONTINENTAL
REFORMERS

THE PROBLEM OF AUTHORITY IN THE CONTINENTAL REFORMERS

A STUDY IN
LUTHER, ZWINGLI, AND CALVIN

BY

RUPERT E. DAVIES
M.A.(OXON.), B.A., B.D.(CANTAB.)

Late Senior Denyer and Johnson Scholar of the University of Oxford
Chaplain of Kingswood School

1946

THE EPWORTH PRESS
(EDGAR C. BARTON)
25–35 City Road, London, E.C.1

All rights reserved
First published 1946

111443

230.032
D 288

*This book is published in complete conformity
with the authorized economy standards*

Made in Great Britain

UXORI CARISSIMAE
CONSILIORUM SOCIAE
LABORUM ADIUTRICI

TABLE OF CONTENTS

PREFACE

THE problem of authority in religion is one of the perennial problems of human thought and experience. This book is an attempt to show how it presented itself to Christians in a particular historical setting, and to discuss the value of the solutions which some of them accepted. Recent theological movements, appearing first in Germany and now spreading over this country, have brought the problem to the forefront once again. It may not be profitless to observe the warring factions on an ancient battlefield from the safe distance of history before choosing our sides and taking up arms in the same struggle now renewed. We may even dare to hope, though it be in the teeth of human experience, to avoid by this means some of the mistakes which our fathers made.

But I do not claim to be above or outside the conflict. Therefore I have tried very hard to keep my historical inquiries into the views of Luther, Zwingli, and Calvin entirely separate from my personal judgement on those views. In this way, perhaps, those to whom my judgements are repugnant will be able to derive some information from my historical inquiries, or at least regard them without undue suspicion.

This book has been written in school holidays during the war. My readers will notice, and judge without harshness, the resultant discontinuities and inconsistencies.

Because of the war, I have not been able to check a few references, originally made in more peaceful times, to books which, as far as I know, reside only in the libraries of German Universities.

I am responsible for the translations from Latin and German, except where the contrary is indicated.

Since I completed the writing of this book, I have read *Martin Luther: Hitler's Spiritual Ancestor*, by P. F. Wiener (Hutchinson, 2s. 6d.). As it covers some of the ground which I cover here, I feel entitled to say that I regard it as for the most part one-sided and unfair. In particular, no one writing an account of Luther's character and career is entitled to ignore, as Mr. Wiener does, his experience of justification by faith and all its implications. He correctly states several of Luther's attitudes, e.g. to the Peasants' Revolt, and to the relationship of the Christian to the

State, but even then he does not give the underlying reasons for those attitudes—and there is a certain inconsistency in a work which begins by maintaining that the conception of Luther prevalent for hundreds of years is legendary, and then asserts that the *real* Luther exercised a profound influence on religion, philosophy, and politics throughout that period.

My warm thanks are due to those who administer the benefactions of Denyer and Johnson in Oxford and John Finch in Wesley House, Cambridge, for making it possible for me to carry out research at the University of Tübingen; to the Professors at that University who helped me with my work; to the Rev. Dr. R. Newton Flew, Principal of Wesley House, who encouraged me throughout and stimulated me into the actual writing of this book by saying that if I waited until I had read every book on the subject I should never write anything at all; to Mr. C. G. Stone, one-time Fellow of Balliol College, Oxford, who read the whole book in typescript with the most scrupulous care and made a very large number of valuable suggestions, both large and small; to my colleagues in the Methodist ministry, the Revs. A. R. George, P. S. Watson, and C. Kingsley Williams, who criticized most usefully parts of the work; to my anonymous examiners for the degree of Bachelor of Divinity in Cambridge, who after approving my thesis made many constructive suggestions for its improvement; to the Rev. J. N. Sanders, Rector of Glaston, and Mr. F. J. Tongue, of Kingswood School, whose help in proof-reading was indispensable; and to my wife, without whose willingness to subordinate domestic urgencies in wartime to the pursuit of truth this book would certainly not have been written.

R. E. D.

Kingswood School
  at Uppingham
    August 1945

INTRODUCTION

THE problem of authority in religion can be stated as follows: is there any accessible source of religious truth which is wholly authoritative? and, if so, what is it? This statement of the problem allows for the possibility that the source may be either inside or outside the human mind; the word 'accessible' means 'capable of being arrived at and understood by the human mind, corporate or individual, assisted or unassisted'; the insertion of the word 'religious' before 'truth' is intended not to imply that there is a distinction between religious and other sorts of truth, but to leave the question open whether there is such a distinction, and to confine the problem to such truth as is ordinarily (whether rightly or wrongly) thought to fall within the scope of religion; 'wholly authoritative' means 'possessing the right to claim universal acceptance of all propositions derived from it, simply because they are so derived'.[1]

This problem is, in an important sense, the central problem of theology. Its solution would put all the other problems of theology on a clearly defined level. Could the wholly authoritative source of religious truth be discovered, the problem of the Atonement, for instance, would be no longer: which is the right theory of the significance of the Cross? But: what is the meaning of the pronouncement of the authoritative source on the subject? And the same, *mutatis mutandis*, would apply to the other problems of theology. In fact, this is precisely what did happen to theology in the Middle Ages to a large extent: the problem of authority was thought to have been solved, and so the theologians applied themselves to the elucidation of the truth thought to have been authoritatively revealed; only thus was made possible the synthesis that Thomas Aquinas achieved.[2] This also is what happens to theology among Fundamentalists today;[3] it is identical with Biblical exegesis. Could it be demonstrated, on the other hand, that there is no wholly authoritative source of religious truth, any

---

[1] It should be noted that when we are led or helped to see something *for ourselves* by someone or something, that person or thing is not, for us, authoritative; we believe something 'on authority' only when we believe it simply because someone or something tells us that it is so.

[2] *vide* Macmurray, *The Clue to History*, p. 161.

[3] And, largely, among modern 'neo-Biblicists', e.g. A. Richardson in *Preface to Bible Study*.

distinction which may be held to exist between theology and philosophy would disappear, and the problems of theology would have been shown to be on the same level as the problems of metaphysics.[1] Until the problem of authority is solved, it is by no means clear what the status of theological problems is. Between the extreme views, one, that they are concerned merely with the elucidation of authoritative pronouncements, the other, that they are purely speculative, there are many mediating views, none wholly satisfactory; if the problem were solved, this issue would be finally settled.

That is the theoretical importance of the problem. Its practical importance is also considerable. In the practical sphere its solution would have at least two results. Firstly, it would put an end to the present conflicts between Churches claiming to represent true Christianity and to proclaim truly Christian doctrines, but differing from each other in life and faith; such conflicts as arose after the solution of the problem would be concerned with the interpretation of authoritative pronouncements, no longer with the claim of this or that Church to contain the source of truth within itself. It would thus tend very strongly in the direction of uniting the Churches. Secondly, having helped to reunite the Churches, it would equip the wholly or partly united Church with the certainty which is at present possessed in full measure only by the Roman Church and the Fundamentalists. Both the former and the latter claim to know the answer to the problem of authority, and the certainty thus engendered has given to the former a power of influence and survival which has stood it in very good stead in a world which has often been exceedingly hostile.

It may be objected that the problem of authority is from its nature insoluble: for if anyone should propound a solution, there would be no reason to ascribe authority to what he had to say, the problem of authority having, up to that point, not been solved. This objection must be upheld in the sense that it must be admitted that no theory of authority can be authoritatively set forth; but it is not necessarily impossible to solve the problem of authority provisionally, in the sense of providing an answer which is consonant with human reason and experience. It is in this sense that an answer to moral problems is sought and often

---

[1]Whether the Christian religion, in any form so far conceived, could survive this demonstration, since it is, apparently, bound up with certain historical events which have to be accepted 'on authority', is another question.

gained. There is reason for hoping, too, that such an answer once gained to the problem of authority would in the course of time command the assent of everyone, in the same way that there is nowadays very little questioning of the proposition that slavery is a moral evil. It is for such an answer, then, that we are to seek.

It is reasonable to expect from the age of the Reformation some help in the discovery of the desired answer, for the question of authority came to the front more prominently in that age than at any other point of history, before or since. It is not too much to say that it was the fundamental issue of the Reformation, although it was by no means always recognized as such by the leaders of the various sides, and still less by their uninstructed followers. The Roman Church had always shown itself able to retain within its ranks men whose type of piety or religious experience was different from the normal and orthodox, and even inconsistent with it; the early monks and the mystics furnish many examples of this. Luther was in the first place not a theologian with a system of Christian belief other than that of the Catholic Church, but a man who had received a vivid experience of Christ, immediately, as he thought, and not through the usual channels. If that experience had not involved for him (only half-consciously at first, as we shall see) a theory of authority in religion which was at variance with the one received by the Catholic Church, he would probably not have become a reformer, certainly not a rebel; and if he had become a reformer, the Church would have had no difficulty in retaining and using his abundant energy for its own purposes. Many men with an experience equally vivid and equally different from the normal, before, during, and after the time of Luther remained without difficulty within the Church; many reformers remained within the Church with only slight difficulty. Ignatius Loyola, whose religious experience strongly resembled Luther's, is an outstanding example of both these statements. But he did not raise the question of authority. Wyclif[1] and Hus[2] did, and so had to be condemned as violently as possible, for they had attacked the foundations of the Church. Luther's theory of authority involved a similar attack and a similar condemnation, and so made him into a rebel. The same is true of Zwingli and Calvin: they lacked, of course, Luther's peculiarly profound religious experience, but they by no means lacked

[1] Explicitly in *de Veritate Sacrae Scripturae* (I, 39, *et passim*) and implicitly in the whole argument of *de Ecclesia*, as well as elsewhere.
[2] e.g. in his *de Ecclesia*, which is almost entirely borrowed from Wyclif's work of the same name.

religious experience altogether, and in their case also it was somewhat different from the normal; yet if they had not arrived at
theories of authority opposed to that of the Catholic Church by
means of the humanistic study of the Bible, they would probably
have become ecclesiastical or secular statesmen, certainly not
rebels. Nor, although nationalistic or other enthusiasms greatly
assisted the progress of the Reformation, would it have finally
succeeded in any country if the leaders had not been able to
proclaim and to put into visible practice a definite theory of
authority to supplant the old. For one of the secrets of the success
of Catholicism has always been, and was in the age of the Reformation, the fact that it can offer to those in perplexity the assurance
of an unquestionable authority, and can promise to its members
that when their faith temporarily fails they can still cling to the
knowledge that the Church cannot be mistaken. The Reformers
could succeed only by providing a substitute for what was
provided by the Roman Church.

From these considerations it seems reasonable to conclude that
the Reformation hinged on the question of authority, and this
conclusion is confirmed by the Protestant Schoolmen's action in
erecting the infallible Bible as the sole and sufficient authority for
Christian belief and practice. It is, moreover, implicitly accepted
by Protestant historians when they call the Bible the formal
principle of the Reformation, and by Catholic historians when
they charge Luther with making private judgement into the
criterion of truth and repudiating the wisdom and authority of
the Church.[1]

We are, then, justified in expecting from the Reformers some
assistance towards the solving of the problem of authority. But
the value of that assistance is diminished at the outset by one
important fact: whereas everyone who reflects nowadays on the
problem must regard as a possible answer the suggestion that
there is no authoritative source of religious truth, no one in the
age with which we are concerned either conceived such a solution or would have considered it for a single moment. All thinkers,
whether they were Catholics, Lutherans, Anabaptists, Zwinglians,
Calvinists, Socinians, or whatever they were, agreed with one
voice that there is an authoritative source of religious truth; the
question that divided them was: what is it? Therefore when we
speak of the answer given by the Reformation and the Counter-
Reformation to the problem of authority, we have to remember

[1] So H. Grisar, *Luther*, I, vi, *passim*.

that this presented itself to them, not in the double form in which it is put on p. 9 above—the form surely in which it should be put—but in the simplified and single form: what is the authoritative source of religious truth?

To investigate the answers given to this by the Reformation, the following method will be employed: we shall take in turn Luther, Zwingli, and Calvin, and ask in relation to each of them three questions: (*a*) To what extent and in what sense did he recognize the problem? (*b*) What answer did he give? (*c*) Will this answer hold? The purpose of the first question is to discover whether the thinker under review faced the problem consciously at all—for our inquiry is partly historical—and if so in what guise we may expect to find the answer given. But if it turns out, in any given case, that the answer to the first question is that the problem was not recognized at all, it will still be necessary to proceed to the second question; for the problem, as we have seen, underlay all the other problems and conflicts of the period, and each man who took a leading part in them was bound to display, in the principles which he embraced and the methods which he adopted, a definite attitude to the problem of authority, even if he never clearly formulated it to himself. It is in any case clearly important to ask the third question, for we are concerned, not merely with an historical question, but with a living issue.

CHAPTER I

LUTHER

I

To what extent, if at all, and in what sense did Luther recognize the problem of authority? We shall answer the first part of this question best by following the development of his relevant theological opinions as far as the point where they can be said to have settled down and become relatively unchangeable. It is, however, unnecessary to take the inquiry back before the first great spiritual crisis of his life, the decision to enter the monastery in 1505, for there is certainly no trace of any tendency whatever before that point to question any of the beliefs in which he had been brought up or which were commonly taught by the Church of the time.

Nor do his early years in the monastery at Erfurt betray any trace of such questioning. It seems very probable that the chief cause of his entering the monastery at all was the sense of guilt before an angry God and the desire to be rid of this fear at all costs. At any rate, he submitted himself to the rigours of the Augustinian discipline with more than the usual conscientiousness, and looked upon them as the correct way of achieving reconciliation with God. He was fully instructed in the principles of Scholastic philosophy, and for two or three years, so far as is known, did not doubt the soundness of the Scholastic method and its results.[1] He was in his own words of later date 'a frenzied Papalist',[2] and this applied both to his intellectual and to his spiritual life.

The conflict began about the time of his ordination; it began in the religious and moral realm, and did not for a long time spread to the intellectual realm. The monastic discipline had conspicuously failed to produce the desired and promised effect; Luther was as much a prey to his fear of God and his consciousness of dreadful guilt as he had ever been, despite his prayers and fastings and self-lacerations. It may have suggested itself to his tortured mind that the method which he was employing was not unquestionably the right one; but he did not bring himself to doubt the traditional scheme of salvation. Thus the conflict was engendered

[1] This is established by Mackinnon, *Luther and the Reformation*, I, 40–3; cf. *Tischreden* (*W.A.*), II, 220: '*cum essem monachus nihil volebam obmittere de precibus*'.
[2] In his Preface to his published works (1545).

by the correctness of the received methods in theory and their failure in practice; and the immediate result of it was to make Luther yet more conscious of his own guilt and yet more convinced that he was not among those predestined to be saved. Gerson alleviated his distress to some extent by showing him that humility in man was the necessary condition of God's activity,[1] but he took the conflict with him, still unresolved, to Wittenberg, whither he went as lecturer in 1508. There Staupitz started the process of his enlightenment by changing for him the significance of the term *paenitentia*;[2] it did not mean the mere performance of good works, said Staupitz, but a certain attitude of mind towards God. Luther spent a good deal of his time working out the full implications of this revelation, and it attained great importance for him in his later thinking; but for the present he returned to Erfurt and lectured on the Scholastic philosophy, particularly that of Occam,[3] without allowing himself more than a few slight criticisms of what the Schoolmen had to say. Thus the conflict and its partial resolution were still, to all intents and purposes, on the religious and moral level only. We still have no hint of a change of theological standpoint, and certainly no sign that he was questioning the authority of Church or Pope.

This is further shown by his own account of his visit to Rome on the business of his Order. He described the eagerness of anticipation with which he approached the city which was the centre of his world. He was grievously astonished and shocked by what he saw on arrival, though no doubt his later accounts of it were coloured by his separation of himself from the things for which it stood, and his vision of it at the time was warped by the austerity which was for him then the essence of religion. But there is no evidence, now that the story of his arising from his knees on the steps of Sancta Sanctorum has been consigned to the world of legend,[4] that he suffered during the visit or immediately afterwards any change of heart or mental attitude. It may well be that the horror induced by the discovery that 'Rome is a harlot: poverty is the only crime'[5] affected him more deeply than he

[1] Mackinnon, op. cit., I, 123. Others doubt this. Luther thought Gerson the 'Doctor Consolatorius', at any rate later on.

[2] *vide* Mackinnon, op. cit., I, 128, and passages there quoted.

[3] *vide* Mackinnon, op. cit., I, 135 sqq.

[4] Preserved Smith, *Life and Letters of Martin Luther*, p. 18, tends to accept this story, but Mackinnon, op. cit., I, 144, disposes of it by quoting a sermon of Luther, delivered on 15th September 1545, which gives an account quite different from that which Paul Luther tells as derived from his father when Paul was eleven.

[5] Preserved Smith, op. cit., p. 144, quotes this from Luther, but gives no reference.

himself realized, and helped him without his knowledge to find his way of release by ridding his mind of the almost superstitious awe with which the thought of the Holy City was clothed. The data collected during his stay in Rome provided, too, much valuable material for later controversy. But as far as he himself knew, he returned to Erfurt in the toils of the same conflict with which he had left it and holding the same views on all major subjects.

From Erfurt, relations with his brethren having become strained, he was transferred soon afterwards to a regular professorship at Wittenberg. It was just after this that the second and greater spiritual crisis of his life took place, his experience of 'justification by faith', which resolved his religious conflict and determined the future course of his life. The date of it cannot be precisely fixed, if indeed it took place on a definite date, but we must place it in the years 1512–13.[1] For our purposes we may notice two things about it, both of which are of the first importance for the understanding of Luther's religion and career. Firstly, he was most profoundly convinced at the time and always afterwards that his salvation was wholly and entirely the work of God and not of man; that neither his spiritual counsellors nor he himself had contributed anything worth mentioning to it. We may quarrel with the correctness of this conviction, but we may not doubt its existence. Secondly, he was just as profoundly convinced that the experience had been exclusively mediated to him by the Bible, in particular Romans i. 17, 18; for many months he had been puzzled and worried by this passage, now he was certain that the true meaning of it had driven itself home to him and that God through it had wrought his salvation. This experience of forgiveness and the free grace of God did not mean, of course, that the devil had ceased to trouble him; it did mean that his attacks were occasional rather than incessant and that the victory over him had to be actualized rather than won.

The conflict in the religious and moral sphere was over; the conflict in the intellectual and theological sphere now began for the first time. It took place between the traditional scheme of doctrine, largely Scholastic, in which Luther had been carefully schooled in the monastery, but which had conspicuously failed in practice to cure his sick soul, and the doctrines involved by the experience of justification. It was not a long conflict, and it ended in favour of the doctrines involved by the new experience almost as

---

[1] *vide* Mackinnon, op. cit., I., 148–51, for a discussion of the date. The passage which he quotes from *W.A.*, XLV, 86 is surely decisive.

B

soon as Luther saw that they were involved. His grasp of Scholastic doctrine had never been anything but academic, and perhaps
had never been complete, for his criticisms of it afterwards were
not always profound; his new experience, on the other hand, had
rapidly penetrated to the depth of his being. Conflict, therefore,
soon gave way to certainty and questioning to affirmation.

As the matter became clear to him, he saw that he objected to
Scholasticism on two main grounds, both involved by what we
have already noted in regard to his experience of justification.
In the first and more important place, the Schoolmen seemed to
him to say that man could earn by his good works the favour of
God. (The charge was not wholly just, for they spoke on the
whole of 'unmerited grace', and Thomas insisted strongly on it;
but they laid an almost equal stress on the duty to do what one
could in order to obtain this grace—Thomas protested against
this—and even Thomas held that *full* salvation was obtained,
after justification, by good works).[1] This alleged view was in
arrant contradiction to Luther's deepest conviction. In the
second place he held that they had substituted 'human teaching'
for 'God's Word';[2] they had built on the findings and theories of
Aristotle, and not on the Word of God to be found in the Scriptures; they had set up as the criterion of religious truth conformity
to the demands of human reason, rather than to the revealed
mind of God. Thus the first objection made them out to be
Pelagian and the second rationalistic.

Theodosius Harnack has suggested that yet a third important
objection was present to his mind, though it is not clearly stated
until later on.[3] He held, according to Harnack, that the Schoolmen argued *a priori* by human reason to the existence and attri-
butes of God, as indeed they did, whereas the correct way was to
argue *a posteriori* from the work of God in the soul to the conclusions involved about His power, wisdom, and love; for we men are
not in a position to climb by means of reason to the investigation
of the divine majesty: God has come down to us in Christ, and
what we have to do is to accept this gift and come to know God
through Christ; all other so-called knowledge is idle and blasphemous speculation. Luther states this view about the knowledge of God very clearly later on: e.g. 'You have often heard
that this canon is to be insisted on in the study of the sacred

[1] *vide* in particular, Holl, *Gesammelte Aufsätze*, I; *Luther*, p. 116.
[2] *Menschenlehre* for *Gottes Wort*.
[3] *Luthers Theologie*, Bk. I, Ch. I, par. 3, pp. 47 sqq.

writings, that we ought to abstain from speculation about God's majesty';[1] and 'God does not wish to be known except through Christ',[2] and it seems to be implied by the views which he held and stated about grace and justification at the time which we are considering (e.g. in the *Psalmenvorlesung*); but it cannot be regarded as certain that he already held it to be an objection to the Scholastic position.

The first of these objections to the Schoolmen shows that he has discarded the authoritative Church teachers of his time (though they were not authoritative in the strict sense, and it was open to the orthodox to question them). The second indicates that he already holds a theory of the final authority of the Scriptures, and the third, if it existed, tends in the same direction, since the knowledge of Christ can come only through the Word and the Sacraments on Luther's view. We shall discuss subsequently what his theory was, and whether it represents his final view on the question of authority. Meanwhile, we notice that it was already very important to him. But he was wholly unaware that his views were in any sense opposed to orthodoxy, or in any sense impugned the credit of Church or Pope. On the contrary, we find him, in his lectures at Wittenberg in the years 1513–16, warmly upholding the authority of the Pope and attacking heretics. He is, in fact, fully of the opinion that the Pope and the leaders of the Church hold the same view about the Scriptures as he does, and takes at their face value all official protestations of loyalty to the Word of God.

His own discovery of inward religion gave him a vantage point from which he was well able to see the defects of externalism, and especially of Indulgences in their less spiritual aspects. So we find him, both in his University lectures and in his practical activities as District Vicar, extremely severe against anything that smacked of reliance on ritual or good works for the favour of God, or of worldliness in spiritual matters. And always his arguments and reforms are based on the Word of God, by which alone principles and practices are to be judged. But there is no trace of any thought that in this he was running counter to received opinions or established authority; he regards himself, quite plainly, as a reformer within the Church, caring for her best interests and destroying the work of her enemies.

His *Römerbriefvorlesung* (1516–17) is chiefly notable as being the best exposition that he has left to us of his doctrine of justification

---

[1] *W.A.*, XL, Part I, 75.   [2] *W.A.*, XL, Part I, 602.

by faith and especially as exemplifying his complete repudiation
of the Scholastic idea that justification can be earned by good
works in any shape or form. But it also expresses accurately his
attitude in the matter under discussion. It is well to remember
that it was delivered not very long before the posting of the
Ninety-five Theses. The high authority which he ascribes to the
Bible is shown by such passages as these: 'the Gospel is not just
what Matthew, Mark, Luke, and John have written. It is the
Word of the Son of God, who became flesh, suffered, and was
glorified—it does not matter whether Matthew or Thomas wrote
it, or what words were used or what language'.[1] Again: 'It is for
this reason that in the prophets he calls [what they say] the voice
of God, that we may accept, believe, yield to and humbly submit
our understanding to every single word, whoever speaks it, as if
God himself were speaking it. . . . For thus, and not otherwise,
shall we be justified . . . .'[2] But he upholds, too, the authority of
the Church. Of heretics he first says: 'A heretic ought to bring
forward such evidence [i.e. many passages of Scripture] of his
teaching and heresy. Let him show where the promise has been
made and by whom. Let him show next through whom it was
given, and, finally, in what Scriptures it was given, that they may
show forth the writings as witnesses. But they care nothing for
these things and say in their folly: we have the truth, we believe
it, we hear it, we pray for it, as if the fact that the teaching seems
to *them* to be from God were enough evidence that it is from God,
and as if it were not necessary that God himself should confirm
his own statement and co-operate with signs following, and with
promises and prophecies preceding.'[3] Then he goes on to state
that the authority of the Roman Church rests on its possession
of the things which the heretics lack—proofs from Scripture, signs
following, etc.: 'For thus was the authority of the Church set up,
even as now the Roman Church holds its authority: those who
preach the Gospel without any defects, preach it without fear of
contradiction.'[4, 5] Of the Schoolmen and their relationship to the
Scripture he says here, curiously enough, not that they neglected
them, but that they paid too much attention to their letter and
too little to their spirit: 'At the same time the Thomists and
Scotists and other sects are carried away by rashness: they defend
what is written and the words of their authors in such a way that

[1] *Corollarium* on *Romans XIII, 4*, II, 11, 31, paraphrased.
[2] *Corollarium* on *Romans III, 22*, II, 89, 32.   [3] On *Romans X, 14*, II, 248, 22.
[4] *secure*.   [5] On *Romans X, 14*, II, 248, 22.

they not only scorn to look for the spirit of them, but destroy it in excessive zeal of reverence, thinking that they have done enough if they hold the words alone without the spirit.'[1] Luther believed them to build on Aristotle rather than the Bible, and, having been reminded that they quote the Bible's authority for their statements, replies that they never get beyond its letter to its spirit.

There is no indication that Luther's attitude to authority had changed when he put up the Ninety-five Theses on the door of the Castle Church in Wittenberg. He put them up for disputation in the regular way, and not as dogmatic statements of unassailable truth. He did so because of his hatred of anything that implied that the divine forgiveness could be attained by an outward act, because of his new conception of the meaning of *paenitentia*, and because he believed that the claims made by Tetzel and others for indulgences were inconsistent with the Scriptures; and any one of these reasons by itself would have been sufficient in his eyes to justify his action. It is thus fair to claim that this action was another based on his conception of Scripture's authority. But he still had no notion that he was attacking the Church or any of its doctrines, and he was for a long time regarded by his own Order, not as by any means a heretic, but as an upholder of one view on a controversial point. We need not doubt his statement made in 1545: 'In these matters I thought myself certain to have the support of the Pope, on whose faithfulness I relied so strongly, who in his decrees most clearly condemns the arrogance of the "quaestors" [as he calls the preachers of Indulgences].'[2] So he says in Thesis 5: 'The Pope neither *wishes* nor is able to remit any penalties except those which he has imposed on his own or the canon law's authority'[3]—as if the Pope had to be defended from those who misunderstood his views and practices (cf. Thesis 42: Christians are to be taught that it is not the mind of the Pope . . .; and Thesis 53: They are enemies of Christ and the Pope, who . . .[4]). Yet at the same time he denies that the Pope has the power of the keys (Thesis 26), and contradicts the doctrine of the *Thesaurus Meritorum*, which was set forth in the Bull *Unigenitus* of Clement VI (1343).[5] But all the time Luther seems unconscious of having contravened the Church's doctrine of authority.

---

[1] *Corollarium* on *Romans VII, 1*, II, 165, 7.

[2] *Lutheri Praefatio ad Opera*, in Kidd, *Documents of the Continental Reformation*, p. 21.

[3] Kidd, op. cit., p. 21   [4] Kidd, op. cit., pp. 23, 24.

[5] Kidd, op. cit., pp. 1 sqq.; cf. especially the statement on p. 2, l. 13 that the *Thesaurus* can never be exhausted *propter infinita Christi merita* with Thesis 58 in Kidd, op. cit., p. 24.

But if Luther was unaware of his true position, the opponents created by his action of 31st October 1517 realized it at once. Tetzel saw that Luther had in effect attacked the Pope's authority,[1] and in his second Disputation (for the Degree of Doctor at the University of Frankfurt-on-Oder), he defends it in no uncertain manner: 'Christians should be taught: (1) Since the authority of the Pope is supreme in the Church and has been set up by God alone, it cannot be restricted or increased by any mere man or by the whole world together, but by God alone. . . . (3) The jurisdiction of the Pope is superior to that of the whole universal Church and Council, and we must obey his statutes in humility. (4) The Pope alone has the right to determine matters of faith; he, and no other, interprets authoritatively the meaning of Sacred Scripture in accordance with his own understanding; he has the right to approve or condemn all the words and deeds of others. (5) The Pope's judgement can scarcely err in matters of faith and those necessary for human salvation. (12) The keys of the Church were given, not to the universal Church, but to Peter and the Pope, and in them to all their successors and to all prelates by derivation from them.'[2] Silvestro Mazzolini of Prierio, usually known as Prierias, was the next to take up the challenge, and he went straight to the point by entitling his treatise *de Potestate Papae* and saying: 'I am about to put your teaching to the acid test, my dear Martin, and I must therefore set down rules and lay foundations. . . . Second Foundation: As the universal Church cannot err in deciding about faith and morals, so also a true Council, doing all it can to understand the truth, cannot err . . .; and similarly neither the Roman Church nor the supreme Pontiff, making his decisions *qua* Pontiff, that is, making pronouncements on the score of his office, and doing all he can to understand the truth, can err. Third foundation: Whoever does not rest in the teaching of the Roman Church and the Roman Pontiff, as being the infallible rule of truth, from which even the Sacred Scripture derives its strength and authority, is a heretic.'[3]

If Luther did not at once realize, after reading these writings, that his views directly contradicted the view on authority taken by the supporters of the orthodox Roman position—though not necessarily held by all members of the Roman Church, as the support given to Luther clearly indicates—he had partly done so

---

[1] This is pointed out by K. Bihlmeyer, *Kirchengeschichte*, III Teil, p. 12. Let credit be given to the unfortunate Tetzel when it is due to him!

[2] Kidd, op. cit., p. 31.

[3] Kidd, op. cit., pp. 23, 24.

before his interview with Cajetan in October 1518. This is Luther's own account of what happened on this occasion: 'I soon asked to be told where I had erred, and said that I was not conscious of any error. Then he brought forward the outrageous Bull of Clement VI, which begins *Unigenitus*, saying that I had asserted against it in Thesis 58 that the merits of Christ were not a Treasury of Merits. He therefore urged me to revoke what I had written. . . . I then replied that I had looked carefully, not only at that Bull of Clement VI, but at the one like it of Sixtus IV, but that it had not enough authority for me, for various reasons, and especially because it misused the Sacred Scriptures . . . and that therefore the Scriptures, which I follow in my Thesis, are to be put wholly above the Bull, and that nothing was proved from it—the opinion of St. Thomas was simply quoted and paraphrased.'[1] We see here that Luther had carefully studied the *Unigenitus*, and was prepared, after full consideration, to place the authority of the Bible above that of the Pope. But he was nevertheless surprised by Cajetan's next assertion: 'Then he began to commend the Pope's authority against me, since it is above a Council, Scripture[2] and everything in the Church. . . . This was new to my ears, and I said that on the contrary the Pope was not above a Council and Scripture.'[3] He does not seem to have realized, despite the words of Tetzel and Prierias, the full extent of the Papal claim to authority until this moment. In his official answer to Cajetan, in the face of this, to him, new assertion of it, he roundly denies the authority and truth of the *Unigenitus*, and states that it is necessary to accept only such Papal Decretals as are consistent with the Scriptures and the earlier decrees of the Fathers. He goes on to say that Papal Decretals had often been corrected by later Popes, and quotes the opinion of Nicholas Tudeschi (1386–1445) that General Councils, and indeed any believer who relies on better authority, are above the Pope.[4]

Luther now at last saw clearly that he had to defend his doctrine of the authority of the Scriptures against the overweening claims of the Pope to be above Scriptures and above Councils. He had for the present no word to say against Councils, and tends

---

[1] Kidd, op. cit., p. 33.

[2] H. Wace in *Principles of the Reformation*, p. 35, says that Rome admitted the Scriptures to be the sole rule of faith until the Council of Trent. But this passage clearly contradicts this view, and Luther and his friends from now onwards regarded Rome as setting the Pope above the Scriptures, though he does in one place admit that the Papists support their case from the Scriptures (*W.A.*, XVIII, 182—1525).

[3] Kidd, op. cit., p. 33.   [4] Kidd, op. cit., pp. 34, 35.

to rely on them for support against the Papal claims, as may be seen from his quotation of Tudeschi to Cajetan, his appeal to a General Council (November 1518), and his Thirteenth Thesis against Eck before the Disputation at Leipzig: 'That the Roman Church is superior to all others is proved from the most futile decrees of Roman Pontiffs, all produced during the last 400 years; against them are the histories approved for 1,100 years, the text of Sacred Scripture and the decree of the Council of Nicea, most hallowed of all Councils.'[1] But there is no evidence that he was willing to defend the authority of General Councils as such, apart from this conformity with the Scriptures. The Disputation at Leipzig showed him that his conceptions of the authority of Scripture involved the denial of the authority of General Councils. He had not come to Leipzig, clearly, with any intention of making this denial, and it was the dexterity of Eck which extorted it from him, but it followed inevitably from his views, and its necessity could not have remained obscure to him much longer. The Disputation as a whole showed that Eck, appreciating the fact that the core of the dispute between Luther and the Pope lay in the question of authority, had intended to press Luther very hard on the point. His success in doing so enabled him to score an argumentative victory, since his opponent was drawn into making admissions that he had never thought to make. But after that, there was no going back on his words, for Luther and he had no difficulty in finding out that he had really meant them.

We can see this from his immediately subsequent writings. At first he did not think it necessary to reply in person to the ungainly attack of the Leipziger Alveld in April 1520 (so ungainly that his own monastery tried to have him forbidden to publish anything more on questions of faith), but when a version of it appeared in German, and so was liable to mislead the uninstructed, he took the opportunity of stating in literary form his considered opinion of the Papal claims in the *von dem Bapstum tzu Rom: widder den hochberumpten Romanisten zu Leiptzck*. Alveld had undertaken to prove from the Canon of Scripture that the Pope possessed divine right, but Luther points out that he had in fact used many arguments based wholly on human reason, and 'a scholar ought to have been on his guard against such ineptitude, and to have established the work or ordinances of God with the Scripture, not with human analogies and worldly reason'.[2] He allows himself, despite the point that he has made, to meet Alveld on his

[1] Kidd, op. cit., p. 46.   [2] *W.A.*, VI, 291

own ground: he denies that it follows that the Church must have one head from the fact, even if it be a fact, that all material institutions have one head, and claims that the analogy thus suggested makes the Church into an external collection of people; he distinguishes the true Church from the Roman Church and claims that Christ is the only possible head of the former. Then he deals with Alveld's Biblical arguments: he says that Aaron is a figure of Christ, not of the Pope, and that the 'Rock' passage in St. Matthew's Gospel, if compared with the passages in which Jesus gives the power of binding and loosing to all the disciples, is seen to mean that Peter received the keys of the kingdom simply as the representative of the *Gemeinde* as a whole. The whole effect of the treatise is to deny that the Pope has any divine right at all; in so far as it makes any positive contribution to the theory of the Pope's position, it suggests that the Papacy has been placed in the world by the wrath of God as a punishment: 'We see that the Pope has full power over all our bishops: this has not come about without divine ordinance, although I observe that it has come about not through the gracious, but rather through the wrathful ordinance of God, who allows it in order to plague the world.'[1] Luther's two final points in the treatise are (*a*) that it is intolerable that the Pope should propound new articles of faith, and (*b*) that he proposes to test everything that the Pope does or says by the Bible ('all that the Pope ordains, does and carries out, I will see to it that I test it previously by the Holy Scripture').[2]

Various passages in the *Reformation Treatises* of the same year, 1520, fully confirm the view that Luther had by now clearly grasped the fact that his doctrine of authority conflicted with the Papal one. In the *an den Christlichen Adel deutscher Nation von des christlichen Standes Besserung*[3] he allows the Pope some kind of general spiritual oversight over Christendom, though he does not specify it and it was probably in his mind very circumscribed; but he launches a very heavy attack against the second of the three 'walls' behind which he charges the Papists with protecting themselves. This wall is the claim: 'No one has the right to interpret Scripture except the Pope.'[4] Against this Luther quotes 1 Corinthians xiv. 30 to show that an ordinary Christian may have a truer message to give than the Pope, and that in this case we must obviously listen to the former; then he goes on: 'Christ also says in John vi that all Christians ought to be taught by God; it might

---

[1] *W.A.*, VI, 321.   [2] *W.A.*, VI, 322.
[3] *W.A.*, VI, 381 sqq.   [4] *W.A.*, VI, 406.

happen that the Pope and his followers were evil and not true
Christians, and had no true understanding, taught to them by
God; why should not a man accept his [i.e. the ordinary
Christian's[1]] interpretation of Scripture in such a case? Has not
the Pope often erred?'[2] The effect of the treatise as a whole is to
deny that the Pope has any greater authority in matters of faith
than a layman; in fact, it shows that he may have even less, if he
is not a Christian and the layman is. The *de Captivitate Babylonica
Ecclesiae*[3] expresses or implies the same view in various places.
At the very beginning of it Luther offers his gratitude to Eck and
Emser for their writings about the primacy of the Pope, for they
have assisted him to a knowledge of further truth: 'To be sure
when I denied that the Papacy had divine right, I admitted that
it had human right. But since I have heard and read the marvellously subtle subtleties of these Trossuli,[4] by which they skil-
fully fabricate their idol (for I am not entirely unteachable in
these matters), I now know for certain that the Papacy is the
kingdom of Babylon and the power of Nimrod, that mighty
huntsman.'

We have seen that it was the Disputation at Leipzig that made
explicit Luther's already implicit view that Councils can err, and
are in any case subordinate in authority to the Scriptures. This
view he has no hesitation in maintaining in his subsequent
treatises. It is true that the chief purpose of the *an den Christlichen
Adel deutscher Nation* is to summon the German nobility to call a
Council, but Luther looks upon the projected Council principally
as a means for achieving the end which the Scriptures have
already shown to be the right one, and not in any sense as an
organ for the discovery or interpretation of truth. Within the
treatise he speaks highly of the Council of Nicea, but perhaps
only because it agrees with him, and was not summoned by a
Pope. But of those called by Popes he speaks very slightingly
indeed; thus he says: 'also when I observe the Councils which the
Pope has called, I find nothing notable about their ordinances'.[5]
So in the *de Captivitate Babylonica* he argues that, although it is
true that the Church is able to distinguish the word of God from
the word of man, it is nevertheless impossible to say in any given

---

[1] That this is the meaning of 'his' is shown by the context and expansions of the
text in later editions.

[2] *W.A.*, VI, 411.   [3] *W.A.*, VI, 497 sqq.

[4] A name given to the Roman cavalry after the conquest by it of Trossulum, an
Etruscan town, and used after the Augustan period of fops and coxcombs.

[5] *W.A.*, VI, 413.

case that the Church has spoken; for those who claim to be the Church may not be part of the Church at all, and may all be in error, 'just as Councils have often erred, especially that of Constance, which erred most impiously of all'.[1]

There is no need to pursue this particular inquiry any farther; for we have reached the point where Luther has become fully and permanently aware of the conflict between himself and the Papacy on the question of authority, and of the opposing claims of the Bible, the Pope, and Councils to be the source and test of religious truth. There is no evidence that his awareness of these things ever diminished, and much evidence that it became, if anything, stronger. This evidence abounds in, for instance, the *de servo Arbitrio* of 1525, the *von den Concilien und Kirchen* of 1539, and the *wider den Bapstum tzu Rom vom Teufel gegrundet* of 1545.

We are therefore in a position to summarize our answer to the first part of the question put at the beginning of this chapter: to what extent, if at all, did Luther recognize the problem of authority? Up to the date of his 'evangelical conversion' in 1512–13 we have no reason at all to suppose that the question of authority ever presented itself to his mind in any shape or form. But the almost immediate result of his experience of justification by faith was the conviction that the Scriptures provide the sole and authoritative source of truth. But this conviction did not bring with it the recognition that the Church as a whole or any important member of it held any different view from his own on the point. This recognition remains absent until after the posting of the Ninety-five Theses. The controversy which this act evoked gradually caused him to realize two things, firstly, that the Pope and his supporters claimed an authority for the Papacy which could in no circumstances be reconciled with the supreme authority of the Scriptures; secondly, that the belief in the supremacy of the Scriptures involved the further belief that Councils were capable of error and had in fact erred. The first realization came just before and during the interview with Cajetan, the second in the course of the Disputation at Leipzig. Both the ideas thus arrived at, though first brought home to Luther by the necessities of controversy, were expressed by him fully and without qualification both in his immediately subsequent writings and from time to time throughout the rest of his life.

[1] *W.A.*, VI, 561.

When we turn to the second part of the question put on p. 15: in what sense did Luther recognize the problem of authority?—or, in other words, how did he formulate it to himself or others?—we need not look farther for the answer than the passages already adduced to show the development of his realization of the problem; for there is nothing on the subject in his other early writings or in his later writings which does anything but confirm the impression created by these. We find then that he recognized the question as being: where shall we find inerrant statements of the truths of religion—in the Papal Decrees, the Decrees of General Councils, or in the Scriptures? It is to be noted that he did not think of looking beyond these three candidates.

But we must at once hasten to add that he never thought of the problem of authority as a problem, properly so-called, at all. For theoretical considerations play no part in his approach to the matter. He nowhere discusses or acknowledges the question whether or not there is a source of authority; he appears nowhere to see that the views that the Papacy or Councils are the supreme source of truth can be argued for in a way that requires logical refutation before they can be properly rejected; he completely fails to suppose that his own view needs careful statement and argumentative justification before it can be expected to appeal to the enlightened judgement of his own and subsequent generations. In other words, the issue was not, for him, one in respect of which two or more opinions could legitimately be held. There was therefore, from his point of view, no need at all for the theretical formulation of the problem, and he did not give one.

It is true that he had to reckon with numerous and powerful opponents. He knew well enough in due course, as we have seen, that his view on authority was rejected out of hand by the recognized teachers of the Church. This situation had somehow to be met, but Luther met it simply and solely by asserting that his view was right and that of his opponents wrong, that the Scriptures were supreme and that anyone who placed anything on a level with or above them was denying Christianity and must be ruled out of court. This attitude sprang immediately out of his immovable conviction that his own religious experience was the true Christian experience and led directly to the knowledge that the Scriptures were supreme; anyone who did not know this lacked the Christian experience, and was probably deceived or bribed by the Pope; but if the truth were asserted effectually enough, and the machinations of the Papacy adequately counteracted, men would enter into the Christian experience and come to know the supremacy of the Scriptures.

Thus Luther recognizes the problem of authority only as one that has been already solved, and formulates it only by answering it in his own way. The question is for him from the start, i.e. from his evangelical conversion onwards, a closed question.

That this is so can be seen from practically every passage in his writings in which he deals with those who have different views from his own. Thus in answering Alveld in 1520 he claims that theological questions should be solved only by reference to the Scriptures; and endeavours to prove this point by adducing a passage from the Scriptures themselves (*W.A.*, VI, 291, quoted on p. 24) *supra*, and continuing from the words there given: 'for it is written, that the divine command is justified in and through itself and not by any external aid'). This is a plain *petitio principii*. Luther would scarcely have been guilty of such false reasoning as this if he had not held it to be self-evident that the Scriptures were supreme and that their supremacy needed no argument to support it.

This high-handed and one-sided way of dealing with the matter has awkward consequences for us as we take up our next inquiry, which is into the question: what answer did Luther give to the problem of authority? For though it is already clear in general terms what his answer is, we have no direct and clearly formulated statement of it, and we are compelled to compose it from a number of unguarded and undefined expressions to be found up and down his writings; we have to do for him what he never did for himself, define his terms and protect him from misunderstanding. It is a great pity that he never set down in plain language what was so obvious to him, but its very obviousness prevented him from doing so. Moreover, we meet from time to time in his writings passages which he never harmonized with his main view simply because he never made it clear to himself what that view was.

II

What was Luther's answer to the problem of authority? The passages already quoted from his writings and sayings (especially *Römerbriefvorlesung Corollarium* on *Romans III, 22*, II, 89, 32, quoted on p. 20; his answer to Cajetan, quoted on p. 23; and the words from *W.A.*, VI, 291, quoted on p. 24, and the practice consistently followed throughout the 'Reformation Treatises' of regarding a

text from the Bible as a sole and sufficient ground for any statement or action, show clearly enough that from his 'evangelical
conversion' until the end of 1520 he ascribed, sometimes to the
'Word of God', sometimes to 'the Scripture' (whether he regarded
these as identical will be later discussed, but he usually wrote and
spoke as if they were), an authority which was above that of the
Pope and Councils, and was, in fact, supreme. It will not take
long to show that he made this ascription consistently until the
end of his life. In 1523, in the *von weltlicher Oberkeit*, he says the
Church commands nothing that it does not know to be God's
Word.[1] In the *das eyn christliche Versamlung odder Gemeyne Recht und
Macht habe* . . . of the same year he asserts that the judgement of
doctrine and the appointment and dismissal of teachers and
pastors must be carried out solely according to the Scripture and
the Word of God,[2] and he commends this work to the public in
his title on the ground that he gives 'Ground and reason from the
Scripture'. In 1524–5, in the *wider die himmlischen Propheten*, he
attacks Carlstadt on the ground that he was forsaking the Scriptures and taking his stand on the grounds provided by Dame
Reason.[3] In 1525, in the *de servo Arbitrio*, he attacks the statement
of Erasmus that he submits himself to the 'inviolable authority of
the Divine Scriptures and the decrees of the Church' on the
ground that submission to the Scriptures is all that is necessary.
for the Church cannot decide beyond what is already decided
in the Scriptures.[4] In 1528 Luther accepts the articles of the
Apostles' Creed because he is convinced that their teaching is
contained in Scripture.[5] In his introduction to the Great Cate-
chism of 1529 he says that everyone ought to know and understand the Ten Commandments, the Apostles' Creed, and the
Lord's Prayer, because they comprise in brief the content of the
Scripture.[6] In 1530 the signatories to the Confession of Augsburg,
written by Melanchthon and heartily approved by Luther, say
that it was produced in order to show that the Protestants believe
nothing which is 'contrary to Scripture and the Catholic Church',
and undertake to provide any further information according to
the Scriptures;[7] the document assumes throughout that Scripture
is the necessary and sufficient ground of any doctrine.[8] In

---

[1] *W.A.*, XI, 262.   [2] *W.A.*, XI, 408, 409.
[3] *W.A.*, XVIII, 182.   [4] *W.A.*, XVIII, 604.
[5] *vide* H. Grisar, *Luther*, II, p. 713, who quotes *W.A.*, XXVI, 500 (from the *Bekenntnis
vom Abendmahl Christi*).
[6] *W.A.*, XXX, Part I, pp. 126–8.   [7] Kidd, op. cit., p. 288.
[8] Kidd, op. cit., pp. 259–89.

1539, in the *von den Concilien und Kirchen*, Luther is concerned, throughout the part relating to Councils, to assert that the sole function of a Council is to reaffirm the doctrines set forth in Scripture,[1] and he willingly admits the possible objection of his opponents that he is leaving no more power to a General Council of the whole Church than is exerted by a pastor or schoolmaster, and claims that a Council does on special occasions exactly what a pastor or schoolmaster does on ordinary occasions.[2]

But, despite the impressive unanimity of this evidence, two questions in this matter still remain. In the first place, it has been asserted by numerous writers, e.g. Grisar,[3] Troeltsch,[4] A. Sabatier,[5] McGiffert,[6] Binns,[7] and J. W. Allen,[8] that to Luther the Word of God and the Scripture were not in all respects identical; we have therefore to ask what it exactly was to which he ascribed such high authority. And, secondly, we must inquire more carefully than we have so far done into the precise nature of this authority, and the kind of submission which its organ demands.

There is no evidence that Luther distinguished between the Scripture (*die Schrifft*, or, of course, *die heilige Schrifft*) and the Word of God before the end of the year 1520. He used the terms interchangeably, and made the same statements about one as about the other. He does not state that they are identical, but assumes it as obvious. If he had been asked why he laid so much emphasis on and ascribed such authority to the *Schrifft* he would undoubtedly have replied in words to the effect that he did so because it was the Word of God; and that would have been for him the end of the matter. In other words, having reached the experience of justification by faith through the instrumentality of certain passages in the Bible, notably some in the Epistle to the Romans, he was thereby led directly to the conviction that the whole Bible possesses *alleinige Autorität;* for he simply accepted, without thinking about the matter, the universal view that the Bible was (*a*) an undifferentiated unity, and (*b*) the Word of God. It would, as a matter of fact, have been extremely strange if he had not done so.

He does not wholly abandon this position in the years after

[1] *W.A.*, L, 547–624.   [2] *W.A.*, L, 614, 615.   [3] op. cit., II, 710.
[4] *Sociallehre der Christlichen Kirchen*, Eng. trans., II, 486.
[5] *Religions of Authority and the Religion of the Spirit*, I, p. 157.
[6] *Protestant Thought before Kant*, p. 56.
[7] *The Reformers and the Bible*, p. 25.
[8] In *The Social and Political Ideas of Some Great Thinkers of the Renaissance and Reformation*, p. 173.

1520, and in most of his arguments from the Bible, which, as we
have seen, are very numerous, there is no sign that he has abandoned it at all. Moreover, in the *de servo Arbitrio* of 1525 he proves
at great length that all parts of the Bible are perfectly clear.[1] He
shows in one place that the meaning of the Scripture is attested
by two witnesses: an internal one, through which, by the help of
the Holy Spirit, every individual Christian can understand, for
himself only, all the Christian doctrines; an external one, by
which we can elucidate these doctrines for the benefit of others.[2]
He then labours to prove, by adducing numerous passages from
all parts of the Bible, that it is clear from beginning to end.[3] The
first of these two arguments fails at any point to make any distinction between the Scripture and the Word of God; the second
definitely assumes that there is no such distinction.

But there are distinct signs of a different, and in those times
revolutionary, view of the matter in writings which had been
published earlier than the one last quoted. The same experience
of justification which had led him to put the Scripture on so lofty
a pedestal led him also to study it with ever greater care, with a
view both to his projected translation of it into the German
tongue and to his own further sanctification. In his study of it
he was constantly looking for the Gospel of justification, and
finding it, too, in the most unlikely places, such as the Book of
Psalms.[4] But in some places, look how he would, he could not
find it, even after the use of those allegorical methods of which
in theory he strongly disapproved. His failure to discover it in
most of the Old Testament did not worry him or affect his views,
for the Old Testament contained the Law, for the natural man,
and could hardly be expected to proclaim the Gospel in the same
breath; the Law comes from God, of course, is eternal, and is
intended to be a παιδαγωγός to Christ, but it is the opposite of
the Gospel, and achieves damnation, not salvation, for it cannot
be fulfilled. It is, in fact, the Word of God, but spoken only to the
natural conscience of humanity.[5] The case was different with
the New Testament, which professed to be concerned with the
Gospel, and was universally held to be apostolic; the absence of
the Gospel from any book of it shocked Luther profoundly, and

---

[1] *W.A.*, XVIII, 606–9 and 652–61.

[2] *W.A.*, XVIII, 653. The 'external witness' is public preaching, thought by Luther
to have a self-authenticating power.

[3] *W.A.*, XVIII, 654–7.   [4] *vide* his second *Vorrede auf den Psalter*, par. 4.

[5] For an exposition of Luther's distinction between the Law and the Gospel, *vide*
P. Schempp, *Luthers Stellung zur Heiligen Schrift*, par. 7.

we may even imagine that the discovery of it caused one or more of the Devil's visits to him in the Wartburg.[1] This pained disappointment accounts for the furious scorn which he vents on the unfortunate Epistle of James both in his *Tischreden* and in his published works.[2] There was only one way of escape for one who based his whole religious experience and his whole movement against Rome on the Scriptures, and that was to set up within the New Testament a criterion by which the claim of any book to be part of the Word of God could be tested. The distinction between the Law and the Gospel, which had worked well enough in the Old Testament, would not here meet the case, for the New Testament had no right to concern itself with the Law. And so the criterion, springing naturally and inevitably out of Luther's fundamental conception of religion, emerged in his mind: does this book preach the Gospel or not? Does it do the works of Christ or not? *Treibt es Christum oder nicht?*—these three questions having exactly the same meaning to Luther. If the answer 'Yes' could be given to these questions in respect of a book, then that book could be thenceforward regarded as evangelic, apostolic, and an integral part of the Word of God (these three terms were not distinguished in meaning when applied by Luther to a book of the Bible); if it could not, then that book possessed no inherent claim on the belief or obedience of a Christian.

This process of thought and its results come out very clearly in the Prefaces which he attached to the New Testament as a whole and to the separate books in his translation of the New Testament, published in September, 1522. The Preface to the New Testament as a whole concludes with a section entitled: 'Which are the true and noblest books of the New Testament'; in it he explains that the Gospel of John, the Epistles of Paul, especially Romans, Galatians, and Ephesians, the First Epistle of John, and the First Epistle of Peter are to be preferred above the other books of the New Testament, because they explain how faith in Christ overcomes sin, death, and hell, and gives life, righteousness, and holiness; these books contain, in fact, all that it is necessary to know for the salvation and sanctification of one's soul. Then he goes on immediately: 'Therefore is St. James's Epistle a right strawy epistle in contrast to them, for it has nothing evangelical about it at all';[3] and promises to explain this point further in other

---

[1] Others ascribe these to ill-health consequent on rich fare: *vide* Preserved Smith, op. cit., p. 125.

[2] *vide infra*, and on p. 34. [3] *eyn rechte stroern Epistel gegen sie.*

C

prefaces.[1] So far Luther has not denied outright that any book is apostolic or part of the Word of God. But he goes much farther in his Prefaces to the later books of the New Testament. At the beginning of the Preface to the Epistle to the Hebrews he says: 'Up till now we have had the true and certain chief books of the New Testament. The four that now follow have from early times had a different reputation.' Then he shows that the Epistle is not the work of Paul or any Apostle, and, in fact, contradicts the Gospel and the Pauline Epistles in one of its doctrines.[2] Yet more definite than this is the *Vorrhede auff die Episteln Sanct Jacobi unnd Judas.* He begins by ascribing to the Epistle of James a measure of faint praise on the ground that it 'sets forth no human teaching and deals strictly with the law of God'. Then he at once states that he does not believe it to be the work of an Apostle, and gives his reasons for this view: firstly, it asserts that Abraham was saved by works, in flat contradiction of all that St. Paul says on the subject of justification; secondly, though it mentions Christ, it gives no teaching about Him, and says nothing about His sufferings and resurrection. Now comes the clearest and most definite statement in the whole of Luther's writings about the relationship between the Word of God and the books of the New Testament: 'The task of a true Apostle is that he preach about Christ's sufferings, Resurrection, and office, and lay the foundation of this faith, as Christ himself says in John xviii, "ye shall bear witness of me"; and all genuine holy books agree in this respect, that they all preach Christ and treat of Him. Moreover, one applies the true touchstone for judging all books, if one sees whether they treat of Christ or not, since all Scripture shows forth Christ (Romans iii), and Paul wishes to know nothing save Christ (1 Corinthians ii). That which does not teach Christ is not apostolic, even if Paul or Peter is the teacher; again, that which preaches Christ is apostolic, even if Judas, Annas, Pilate, and Herod do the preaching.'[3] Of the Epistle of Jude he says in the same preface that it is clearly an abridgement of 2 Peter and need not be reckoned among the 'chief books which are to lay the foundations of the faith'.[4] In the Preface to the Apocalypse he says that the book is certainly not apostolic (here, probably in the

---

[1] *W.A.*, Deutsche Bibel, Bd. 6, p. 10. Preserved Smith (op. cit., p. 268) ascribes this Preface to 1545 instead of 1522; actually it was omitted from the 1545 edition. The editor of the *W.A.* volume just quoted suggests that Luther's antipathy to the Epistle of James was partly due to Carlstadt's admiration for it.

[2] *W.A.*, Deutsche Bibel, Bd. 7, p. 344.   [3] *W.A.*, Deutsche Bibel, Bd. 7, p. 384.

[4] *W.A.*, Deutsche Bibel, Bd. 7, p. 386.

sense of 'written by an Apostle'), on the ground among others that Christ is not preached in it, and although a later Preface which was substituted in 1530 for that of 1522 somewhat modifies the low opinion of the book expressed in the latter, yet Luther was still quite unconvinced when he wrote the later Preface that the book was apostolic.[1] By way of contrast to his views on these four books, the Preface to the Epistle to the Romans may be quoted, as showing almost as clearly the nature of the criterion which Luther employed for differentiating between the books of the New Testament; he begins by saying: 'This Epistle is the true masterpiece of the New Testament and the purest Gospel of all, deserving indeed that a Christian should not only know it by heart, but should treat it daily as if it were the daily bread of the soul; for it can never be too much or too well learned or considered; the more it is used, the more precious it becomes', and then he launches into an enthusiastic review and elucidation of the book's contents; finally he says: 'So we find in this Epistle in the most abundant fashion that which a Christian ought to know, viz. what are Law, Gospel, Sin, Punishment, Grace, Faith, Righteousness, Christ, God, Good Works, Love, Hope, the Cross. . . . Therefore it seems as if St. Paul wanted briefly to summarize in this Epistle the whole of Christian and evangelical teaching, and to provide an introduction to the whole of the Old Testament. For, without doubt, whoever has this Epistle well in his heart, has with him the light and strength of the Old Testament.'[2] It is evident from this and the preceding exposition that Luther's reason for regarding the Epistle to the Romans as the 'true masterpiece' of the New Testament is that it contains in undiluted form the Gospel of justification, especially when we read this Preface in the light of those to the Epistles of James and Jude.

W. Heinsius claims[3] that Luther grounded his distinction between the 'true and certain chief books' of the New Testament and its four last books on the opinion of Eusebius of Caesarea that the inclusion of the latter in the canon of the New Testament was problematic. Heinsius does not quote the passage or passages in which Luther adduces Eusebius; but Luther, in the Preface to the Epistle to the Hebrews, does say that Hebrews, James, Jude, and the Apocalypse 'have from early times had a different reputation';[4]

[1] *W.A.*, Deutsche Bibel, Bd. 7, pp. 404 sqq.

[2] *W.A.*, Deutsche Bibel, Bd. 7, pp. 1–26.

[3] In a footnote on p. 105 of his edition of the *Vorreden zur Heiligen Schrift* (Kaiser, München, 1934).

[4] *W.A.*, Deutsche Bibel, Bd. 7, p. 344.

and in the Preface to the Apocalypse (1522) he gives the doubts of
Jerome as one of the reasons for questioning the apostolic character
of the book.[1] But the whole tone of the Prefaces shows that the
argument from the Fathers occupies a very subordinate position
in Luther's mind, and was, in all probability, an afterthought;
it is not mentioned at all in the all-important Preface to the
Epistles of James and Jude. The very minor part played by it in
Luther's mind and the all-sufficiency of the test 'Does this book
preach Christ or not?' are admirably shown in a passage from the
Tischreden quoted by Preserved Smith,[2] in which the reference to
the opinion of the Fathers is merely tacked on to Luther's real
reasons for rejecting the Epistle of James: 'Many sweat to reconcile St. Paul and St. James, as does Melanchthon in his *Apology*,
but in vain. "Faith justifies" and "faith does not justify" contradict each other flatly. If anyone can harmonize them I will
give him my doctor's hood and let him call me a fool. Let us
banish this epistle from the university, for it is worthless. It has
no syllable about Christ, not even naming him except once at the
beginning. I think it was written by some Jew who had heard of
the Christians but not joined them. James had learnt that the
Christians insisted strongly on faith in Christ and so he said to
himself: "Well, you must take issue with them and speak only of
works", and so he does. He says not a word of the Passion and
Resurrection of Christ, the text of all the other Apostles. Moreover, he has no order nor method. . . . The ancients saw all this
and did not consider the epistle canonical.' From all this it
appears that Heinsius needs to produce a very definite passage or
series of passages from Luther if he wishes to show that Luther
set any store by the argument from Eusebius or any of the
Fathers.

We conclude therefore that from 1520 onwards Luther was very
liable to speak and write in his unguarded moments as if he
identified the text of the Bible with the Word of God; but that
when he applied himself carefully to the study of the Bible and
published the results of that study he concluded that within the
New Testament the books were each to be tested by the criterion:
does it preach the Gospel of justification or not? with the corol-
lary that those about which the answer 'No' had to be given were
not to be regarded as part of the Word of God. In Luther's

---

[1] *W.A.*, Deutsche Bibel, Bd. 7, p. 404.

[2] op. cit., p. 269 (owing to P. Smith's regrettable habit of not giving his references,
the passage must here be given without date or reference).

deliberate opinion, then, the Old Testament consists partly of the Law and partly of the Gospel, both of which are parts of the Word of God to men;[1] the New Testament consists partly of the Gospel, in fact, mainly of the Gospel, which is part of the Word of God, and partly of books which do not set forth the Gospel and are not parts of the Word of God.[2,3]

This view was new in two senses. The Synod of Carthage in 397 fixed the canon of the Old and New Testaments, and since that event no responsible Christian had ventured to suggest that any book thus canonized was not a true part of Scripture. Theodore, Bishop of Mopsuestia from 392 to 428, certainly held at one time that Job and the Song of Songs formed no true part of the Old Testament and the Catholic Epistles no true part of the New,[4] but we are to presume that he submitted to the decision of the Synod, since he was not condemned until 553 (though his views on the Bible were reckoned then among the charges against him); he therefore does not count as a true exception, and in any case his antiquity would make him no more than a technical one. Luther, then, was the first who dared to suggest that the ratified decision of the Church on the point was questionable, but as he had already asserted that many other ratified decisions of the Church were questionable, this was perhaps not so great a matter. His other innovation was a much more important one. Among others, Origen,[5] Dionysius of Alexandria,[6] and Theodore of Mopsuestia had, before the Synod of Carthage, doubted the canonicity of books afterwards included in the Old and New Testaments. But these and the others give for their doubts grammatical, literary, historical grounds. Luther on the other

[1] It would not have been surprising, in view of the historical mistakes which he ascribes to certain parts of the Old Testament, and his modified praise of the prophets, if he had said that certain books of the Old Testament were not part of the Word of God. But he does not seem to do so.

[2] cf. W. P. Paterson, *The Rule of Faith*, Appendix E. He gives much of the evidence given here, but does not draw the same conclusions.

[3] It should be pointed out here that Luther uses the term 'Word of God' in two other senses also than the one defined in the last few pages: (*a*) to signify the *meaning* of the Word of God in the sense already defined, summed up (*W.A.*, XXIII, 183—1527) as: 'Christ, God's Son, is our Saviour'; (*b*) to signify Christ, the living Word of God. It is clear that both these additional senses tend sometimes to run into the sense already defined, but they do not exert enough influence on it to affect Luther's doctrine as here given, though they enable him sometimes to transcend in practice and devotion the literalism of his theory and usual practice.

[4] *vide* Kidd, *A History of the Church*, III, 197.

[5] *vide* e.g. in Eusebius, *H.E.*, VI, xxv, 11–14 (No. 124 in Kidd's *Documents Illustrative of the History of the Church*), where he discusses the authorship of the Epistle to the Hebrews.

[6] *vide* 'On the Promises' in Eusebius, *H.E.*, VII, xxv, 17–27 (No. 165 in Kidd's *Documents*), where he discusses the authorship of the Apocalypse.

hand gives purely religious grounds. That is to say, he takes for granted a certain content of religious faith (actually that to be found in the Epistle to the Romans), and tests by it all claimants to a place in Holy Writ; those who contradict it he regards as having ignominiously failed the test. This is not quite the same as the modern method of testing all parts of the Scripture by their conformity with the content of faith thought to have been revealed in the life and teaching of Jesus, but it is analogous to it.

It is asserted by Troeltsch,[1] A. Sabatier,[2] J. W. Allen,[3] and Nagel[4] that Luther's views on this point became narrower in his old age, and that he tended then to identify the Word of God with the text of the Bible; Allen, for instance, gives 1530 as the date of this change. But none of these scholars,[5] on whom the onus of proof plainly rests, gives any evidence for his statement.[6] It seems to be the case that there is no positive pronouncement of Luther available from the years after 1530 which distinguishes the Bible from the Word of God, but this fact does not by any means prove that he had ceased to distinguish them; we have seen that even at the time when in his prefaces to the books of the Bible he carefully proves that certain books of the New Testament are not apostolic, in other works he speaks as if there were no distinction at all between the Bible and the Word of God. It is true that in the 1534 edition of the Translation of the Bible he omits from the Preface to the whole New Testament the concluding section entitled: 'Which are the true and noblest books of the New Testament.' But he does not omit the far more definite sentences in the Prefaces to the Epistle to the Hebrews and the Epistles of James and Jude, and these remain also in the edition of 1546. It seems reasonable, therefore, in the absence of evidence to the contrary, to infer that Luther did not abandon the distinction between the various books of the New Testament, but did not trouble to formulate it explicitly any longer, and continued his habit of speaking as if he did not believe in its existence. But, however this may be, we have good reason to regard the view expressed in the prefaces as the one that does most justice to Luther, for it is impossible not to see the signs of weariness and waning powers not long after 1530.

[1] op. cit., II, 486.   [2] op. cit., I, 159.   [3] op. cit., p. 173.

[4] *Zwinglis Stellung zur Schrift*, Introduction.

[5] Nagel *may* give some evidence, but it is impossible at present to find this out.

[6] It is not possible to prove anything from Luther's insistence on the literal meaning of 'This is My body' throughout the controversy with Zwingli and at the Marburg Conference (1529), for such literalism was usual with him at all stages of his career.

We come to the next question: what is the precise nature of the authority which Luther ascribes to the Word of God defined as we have seen that he defined it? Because Luther refused the title of 'Word of God' to various books which were part of the generally accepted canon and therefore certainly did not hold the text of the Scriptures to be infallible, it has often been asserted that he believed in the existence of no infallible organ of authority, and, in fact, rejected the notion of infallibility altogether. A. Sabatier, for instance,[1] points out, quite rightly, that he set up a criterion for the criticism of the Biblical books, and indicates what that criterion was. Then he says, by way of an inference from this: 'The Reformers, and Luther in particular, dreamed of anything rather than of raising up an exterior authority, infallible like that of the Church.' But this is, surely, a confusion of thought. It is quite true that Luther did not substitute an infallible Bible for an infallible Church. But it cannot be inferred forthwith that Luther set up no infallible authority at all. Sabatier also says[2] that Luther 'established a new conception of religion by removing the seat of religious authority . . . from the Church to the Christian consciousness'. This was, no doubt, the underlying tendency and ultimate effect of his work. But it cannot be shown to have been his purpose.

The truth of the matter seems rather to be this. Luther arrived at his high regard for the authority of the Bible as a result of his religious experience of justification by faith. Armed with this experience, he studied the Bible carefully, and discovered that it did not at all points tally with his experience of Christ; he thereupon ceased to identify the Word of God with the Bible, for the Word of God was that which tallied with his experience. But he did not put it to himself like that; what he thought and said was: the Word of God is that which preaches the Gospel—which is an entirely different method of formulation and statement. And at the end of the process the Word of God, as specified by him, emerges in his mind as an infallible, external authority. Luther 'removed the seat of religious authority from the Church' —yes, but not to the Christian consciousness, but to the Word of God. This is shown partly by the fact that, whenever he wishes to prove a point, he always argues from the Bible (never from his own experience of Christ); and still more conclusively from the general tenor of his writings as a whole, and especially from that of the *wider die himmlischen Propheten* (where he is arguing

[1] op. cit., I, 160.   [2] ibid.

against Carlstadt, the prophet of inward illumination), the first part of the *de servo Arbitrio*, and the *von den Concilien und Kirchen*.[1]

The Word of God, then, is infallible—which is, after all, what it might have been expected to be. Its writers, though they remained free personalities when they wrote, were nevertheless preserved by the Spirit from writing what was false. They did not, between them, write the whole truth, for in many matters they do not inform us, and in such matters we are free to think and act as seems right to us;[2] but they did not write anything but the truth. Luther is able to think and say this in spite of the historical inaccuracies which he observed in parts of the Old Testament; presumably he was able to forget these, or to neglect them without any feeling of inconsistency.

The Word of God is also external, objective. It is not stored up in the mind of God, or in nature, to be revealed gradually to the inquiring mind and spirit of man; it is not latent in the human mind and conscience to be elicited by education or illumination. It is written down, once and for all, in the pages of the Bible, and all can read it there. The meaning of the Word of God is perfectly plain throughout,[3] and is agreed on by all whose minds are not corrupted by the Papacy's heresy and ambition. The Christian preacher, while he preaches, is the Word of God in bodily form, so long as he preaches the true Gospel; and while he does this we must submit to him and obey him as we would the Word of God. But the Word of God, written in the Bible, is there to test him and judge him, and, if he contravenes it, to act through the *Gemeinde* and dismiss him.[4]

To this infallible, external authority every man must wholeheartedly and wholemindedly submit, as an individual, as a member of a family, as a member of the Church, and as a member of the State. As an individual he must subordinate all his thinking to the truths set forth in the Word of God.[5] His only method of attaining personal salvation is by having faith in Christ according to the teaching set down in the Word of God. His calling in life has been given to him by God, as is shown in the Word of God, and the Word of God also shows that he must fulfil it, not strive to

---

[1] If further evidence is needed, the passages quoted on pp. 40–47 and 51–53, *infra*, provide it in abundance.

[2] *W.A.*, XVIII, 110 (1525).

[3] *W.A.*, XVIII, 606–9, and 652–61 (1525); *vide supra*, p. 32.

[4] *W.A.*, XI, 411 (1523).

[5] *W.A.*, XVIII, 604 (1525).

change it.[1] This applies even to serfs and slaves.[2] In short, except
in those matters where the Word of God gives no explicit instruction, each man's individual life is controlled and dominated by the
Word of God.

The same applies to a man as a member of a family (in the
narrow sense, not in the wide sense, including all social and
economic relationships, which Luther often gives to the word
Familie). The purpose of marriage is the procreation of children
and the continuance of the human race. It existed in Paradise
with this purpose before the Fall, but the latter event introduced
sexual desire, or rather lust, into the human heart. This, in its
origin and nature, is an evil, but for us the inevitable thing;
God after the Fall arranged that marriage should give it a reasonable cloak and a proper outlet.[3] It is each man's duty therefore
to enter into the married state and to remain faithful to it.
Adultery is not only in itself a sin against God, but it is just as much
a refusal to follow the calling appointed by God as an attempt on
the part of a shoemaker to make himself into a bishop. All these
principles and precepts are laid down by the Word of God,
and it is this fact which makes it obligatory on us to carry them
out.[4] Similarly, the duties of parents to children, of children to
parents, and of husbands to wives are laid down expressly in the
Word of God, and we are therefore obliged to carry them out.
Thus all a man's family relationships are regulated and ordered
by the Word of God.

We are not surprised, therefore, to find that the Word of God
also controls a man as a member of the Church, and the Church
as a whole. Luther, as Holl has convincingly shown,[5] had clearly
formulated to himself the main principles of his doctrine of the
Church as early as his *Commentary on the Psalms* (1513), and

---

[1] For this fundamental idea of Luther's sociological ethic, see, for instance, *W.A.*,
XXX, Part 2, p. 112: 'I want to have the callings and professions clearly distinguished
and separated, so that everyone may see to what he is called by God, and may follow
and do justice to that calling loyally and sincerely, to the service of God.' Luther does
not here cite Scriptural authority, but the quotation in the next note, on similar lines,
does.

[2] So, discussing the Peasants' Articles, he says: ' "There ought to be no serfs because
Christ has set us all free." What, then, is that? This means that Christian freedom
would be quite carnal. . . . Read St. Paul and what he teaches about servants, who in
his time were all slaves. Therefore this article is clean against the Gospel. . . .' (Quoted
by Troeltsch, op. cit., II, 871, from *B.A.* [*sic*], IV, I, 334 sqq.)

[3] See Troeltsch, op. cit., II, 864 (note 258).

[4] *vide* e.g. Luther's arguments, all based on the Word of God, in the *von Ehesachen*
(1530, *W.A.*, XXX, Part 3, pp. 198–248), which is chiefly about betrothals and
divorce.

[5] op. cit., pp. 288–99.

in this he says that the Word of God produces the Church; 'The Scripture is the womb from which are born theological truth and the Church';[1] and again: 'Because the Church is built on the word of the Gospel, which is the word of God's wisdom and virtue.'[2] He says also that the Word preserves the Church: 'The Word of God preserves the Church of God.'[3] This view appears from time to time throughout his writings, for instance in the *de Captivitate Babylonica*, 'The Church is brought to birth by the word of promise through faith, and is nourished and preserved by the same, that is, it is set up through the promises of God, not the promises of God through it,'[4] and remained central to Luther for the rest of his life. In virtue of this he is able to say, as he does in the words immediately following those just quoted: 'The Word of God is incomparably above the Church.'

But, for the sake of intelligibility, some account ought to be given of the Church thus created by the Word, and this can best be done by comparing and contrasting Luther's view of the Church with that of Augustine, from which it was in large part derived. Augustine's view took shape in his mind as he gradually emancipated himself from Manichaeism and Neo-Platonism, but its outlines were sharpened and its content filled out by his controversies with the Manichees, the Donatists, and, to a lesser degree, the Pelagians. In its final form it was something like this: the true, eternal Church is invisible, and unknowable except to God (it is sometimes, but not constantly, called *civitas Dei* in contrast with *ecclesia*, the visible Church). It consists of those created, immortal beings, angels and men, who are called *sancti*, saved or to be saved. It includes, besides the angels who did not fall, some human beings who lived before the Incarnation—Jews[5] and others.[6] This conception of the invisible Church takes its rise from and is rooted in Augustine's doctrine of Grace and Predestination; for it is by the eternal decree of God's Grace, and by that alone, that the number and personnel of the invisible Church are determined. Yet, although the invisible Church is the true Church, there is a sense, as Holl has pointed out,[7] in which it is not a genuine Church at all: for God's decree of election concerns only the individual as an individual, and furnishes no bond of connexion between those who are elected.

---

[1] *W.A.*, III, 454, 25.   [2] *W.A.*, IV, 189, 34.
[3] *W.A.*, III, 259, 18.   [4] *W.A.*, VI, 560.
[5] *de Civ. Dei*, XVI, 3.   [6] ibid., XVIII, 47.
[7] op. cit., p. 299.

This invisible Church corporealizes itself on earth in the institution founded by Christ, which is Christ's instrument for the
instruction and salvation of men, or rather of those men who are
included among the *sancti*. It is the *civitas Dei peregrinans in terris;*[1]
but just as in Israel there were those who were Israelites 'in the
flesh only, and not in faith',[2] so there are many in the visible
Church who are not *sancti*[3]—they will be separated out at the Last
Judgement. Nevertheless, the Church on earth is a branch or part
of the invisible Church (Augustine always avoided the temptation, which must have been strong during the Donatist controversy, of completely identifying the Church on earth with the
true Church); and as such it has certain distinguishing 'marks'
which all men can see—catholicity (on which he very strongly
insists), historical continuity manifested especially in the Apostolic
Succession, and the bond of love.[4]

Luther takes over from Augustine the distinction between the
invisible and the visible Churches. The invisible Church to him,
as to Augustine, is eternal in the heavens, knowable only to God.
But, for Luther, its number and personnel are determined, not
by the eternal decree of God's predestinating grace, but by the
activity of the Word of God in this world; for the Word is double-
edged in its operation, dividing mankind into those who hear and
obey and those who hear and do not obey, as he says already in
the *Commentary on the Psalms* ('the Word of God is a sword, and
the staff of judgement, distinguishing men'),[5] and as he always
maintained. Since the Word of God always binds men together in
fellowship, the invisible Church is a true fellowship. Luther held,
with Augustine, that this invisible Church corporealizes itself in
the world, and that what is called the Church in the world
contains many who have not really heard and obeyed (this view
also appears as early as the *Commentary on the Psalms:* 'speaking
about the double generation of men in the Church, that is, the
carnal and the spiritual'[6]). But Luther drew from the second of
these two contentions a conclusion which Augustine did not draw,
that the visible Church, which is the only true fellowship on earth,
and a reflection of the perfect fellowship of the Church in heaven,
is visible not to all men, but only to those who have the necessary
spiritual vision. Those who have this recognize the visible

---

[1] Holl claims (ibid.) that Augustine never really established the connection between
the invisible and visible Churches.

[2] Augustine, op. cit., XVII, 16.   [3] ibid., XVIII, 48, 49.

[4] *vide* fully, F. Hofmann, *Der Kirchenbegriff des Heiligen Augustinus.*

[5] *W.A.*, III, 348, 21.   [6] *W.A.*, IV, 187, 6.

Church by certain 'marks' or 'signs', which are different from the 'marks' of the Church which Augustine gives. In the *von dem Bapstum zu Rom* he gives these 'marks' as 'Baptism, Sacrament, and Gospel';[1] but by the time of the *von den Concilien und Kirchen* he has elaborated these into seven: the Word of God rightly preached, the Sacrament of Baptism rightly administered, the Sacrament of the Altar rightly administered, the power of the Keys rightly exercised, pastors and preachers rightly called, public prayer and praise, Christians suffering according to the example of Christ.[2]

These signs were most plainly visible, in Luther's opinion, in the Protestant *Gemeinden* set up in Germany and elsewhere in accordance with the principles of his Reformation, and of course also in the early, especially the primitive, Church. But Luther is careful not to deny that they are also present among the Papists, whom he never once describes as heretics as a body or excludes from the true Church as a body; and in one place he expressly admits that the Roman Church is holy: 'the Roman Church is holy, because it has the holy Name of God, Baptism, the Word', and that the Church exists among the *Schwärmer*: 'the holy Church exists among the fanatics, except among those who deny Sacraments and Word'.[3] This is enough to show that Luther did not regard a community where the necessary signs were present as consisting necessarily of no one except true Christians; so naïve a belief, if Luther ever held it, was quickly banished by the conduct of members of some of his *Gemeinden*, and not least of the 'mother-church' of Wittenberg, of which he sometimes doubted whether it was a true *Gemeinde* at all.

For practical purposes, however, the Protestant *Gemeinden* could be regarded, and were regarded by Luther, as not only parts of the true Church, but also as consisting of 'true Christians', each a priest, with direct access to God. It is these whose rights and privileges he describes, and whose constitutions he draws up in detail, and it is these which he really has in mind when he speaks of the Church of Christ as something existing in the world.

Such, then, is the Church created by the Word of God, invisible to the natural eye, but visible to the eye of faith, and such are its component parts; here, then, we may return to our main theme, and disclose how the Church is not only created and sustained, but also regulated and controlled by the Word of God. This comes

---

[1] *W.A.*, VI, 301.   [2] *W.A.*, L, 628–43.

[3] *In Epistolam S. Pauli ad Galatas Commentarius* (1531), *W.A.*, XL, Part 1, pp. 69, 71.

out very clearly indeed in the whole argument and tone of the
das eyn christliche Versamlung odder Gemeyne . . . (1523).[1] This begins
with a statement that there is a *christliche Gemeinde* wherever the
Word is preached, for it is impossible for the Word to be preached
without the result that some men become Christians and form a
Gemeinde. Then it proceeds to state that in such a *Gemeinde* doctrines must be judged, and pastors appointed and dismissed, not
according to human laws or doctrines, but according to 'the
Scripture and the Word of God'. Then Luther proves that the
Word of God, in particular such passages as 'my sheep know my
voice' (John x. 4), gives every Christian the right to judge the
teaching which is provided for him; then, that he has the right,
given to him by the Word, to preach himself when there is no other
Christian to do it; when there are people especially qualified to
preach and teach, to appoint them as preachers and teachers, and,
if necessary, afterwards to dismiss them. Thus the *Gemeinde* is not
autonomous; its considerable rights are wholly derived from the
Word of God. Of course, too, when it exercises its right of criticizing the teaching which is given to it and those who give it, its
touchstone must always be the Word of God, not the personal
views of the *Gemeinde* or any of its members.

It might have been expected that Luther's conception of the
priesthood of all believers would have led him to modify this
view; for it sometimes causes him to speak as if every Christian,
in virtue of his priesthood, were almost a law unto himself; in one
place he proves, for instance, that each believer may perform all
the functions normally belonging to the priest's office, including
not only the celebration of the Eucharist, but also judging every
man's teaching.[2] It is true that he limits this elsewhere by saying
that a Christian may not use his high powers except 'by agreement of the community or at the call of his superior',[3] but it
might have been thought that a community consisting of people
with such high privileges, and itself collectively possessing the
right of outweighing the beliefs of individual members, would be
allowed an independent status of some sort. But this can nowhere
be shown to be the case, and it is highly significant that the very
treatise which is written to show the great powers of the *Gemeinde*
derives them entirely from the Word, and says practically nothing
about the priesthood of all believers (this appears only as one of

[1] *W.A.*, XI, 408–16.

[2] *W.A.*, XII, 180, 1 sqq. (1523); cf. VIII, 248, 2.

[3] *W.A.*, VI, 566, 27 (*de Captivitate Babylonica*); cf. X, Part 3, pp. 97, 1.

the things in virtue of which the Christian has a right to preach
when there is no one else to do it; and even here the more
important ground is the Scriptural one).

There are two passages in Luther's writings which appear to
give to the Church a teaching authority inconsistent with all the
views which we have so far ascribed to Luther on the question
of authority. The first is in the *de Captivitate Babylonica:* 'The
Church certainly has this power, that it can distinguish the Word
of God from the words of men, as Augustine confesses when he
says that he was moved to believe the Gospel by the authority of
the Church, which preached that this was the Gospel—not that it
is therefore above the Gospel (otherwise it would be above God
also, who is the object of faith, simply because it preaches that this
is God), but rather, as Augustine says elsewhere, the soul is so
captured by truth, that it can judge through it most certainly
about all things, but cannot judge the truth itself, but is forced by
infallible certainty to say that this is the truth.'[1] Here Luther
plainly says that the Church can distinguish between the Word of
God and the words of man, because the truth of the Gospel has
compelling power. Taken strictly, this implies that the Church
has an unqualified right and power to distinguish truth from false-
hood, and if this is so, the statement that the Word regulates the
Church falls to the ground, for how can the Word of God be discovered before the Church is there to distinguish it from the
words of men? But Luther has said immediately before this passage that the Word of God is incomparably above the Church, he
says in the course of the passage that his argument does not put
the Church above the Gospel, and he goes on immediately after
the passage to contradict it by saying that the Church has no
right to promise grace or institute sacraments. So that there is
no need to take the passage very seriously.[2]

The second passage is in the *de servo Arbitrio*, and in it Luther
denies that God has tolerated error in the Church; for the Church
'is ruled by the Spirit of God'. Then he quotes with approval the
phrase, 'so that it is impossible for it to err even in the smallest
article', and goes on to maintain that the official Church has

---

[1] *W.A.*, VI, 561, 3 sqq.

[2] It has been suggested to me by Mr. C. G. Stone that what Luther meant was that
a Church that was really a Church would understand the meaning of the Word of
God, and would be aware that the Word of God was the Word of God, and that this
might be a help to individuals, e.g. an individual who noticed that the preachers
of the *Gemeinden* in his neighbourhood thought little of the Epistle of St. James and
much of the Epistle to the Romans might be *helped* to discriminate the Word of God
from the words of men, 'moved by the authority of the Church'.

erred, but that the true Church cannot possibly have done so.[1] This doctrine of the infallibility of the Church comes strangely from the pen of Luther, but the oddity disappears when the words here quoted are taken in conjunction with some earlier words in the same treatise, in which Luther says that the Church can decide nothing save what has already been decided by the Word of God.[2] It is clear, then, that the infallibility of the true Church consists in this, that it unfailingly preaches the truths revealed in the Word of God, and while it does this it cannot be mistaken.

These two passages, then, do not compel us to doubt that the teaching authority of the Church as well as its constitution is derived from the Word of God. That it is so derived is plainly stated in many passages. It suffices here to refer to the passages quoted on pp. 30 and 31 from the *von weltlicher Obrigkeit* and the *von den Concilien und Kirchen*, together with the general tendency of the passages just quoted from the *de Captivitate Babylonica* and the *de servo Arbitrio*.

Thus the Church is brought into being by the Word, preserved by the Word, regulated in its organization by the Word, and controlled in the content of its faith and in its thought by the Word. What applies to the Church as a whole applies to each individual *Gemeinde*, and to each man and woman as a member of a *Gemeinde* and through it of the universal Church.[3]

As an appendix to this description of the subordination of the Church to the Word of God, a long controversy may be briefly noted which concerns the question of what Luther thought that this subordination meant in practice. The organization of the Church, according to Luther, must be determined by the Word of God, and the meaning of the Word of God, again according to Luther, is plain throughout to all who have the eyes to see it and the illumination of the Spirit to help them. The proper organization of the Church should, then, have been easily discernible by all Christians and by Luther himself. But in respect of one aspect of Church government, the relation between Church and State, always important, and particularly important in the period of the

---

[1] *W.A.*, XVIII, 649, 650.   [2] *W.A.*, XVIII, 604.

[3] It is important to notice, however, that Luther did not always in actual practice derive all his beliefs from the Word of God, but sometimes some of them from the universal tradition of the Church. His 'personal confession' at the end of his *Bekenntnis vom Abendmahl* (*W.A.*, XXVI, 499–509—1528), an exposition of the Apostles' Creed, is not only charged with Chalcedonian orthodoxy (which he no doubt believed to be derived from the Word of God), but also approves of the Confessional, without giving or suggesting any Scriptural grounds, but relying on its usefulness and, presumably, the *praxis Ecclesiae*.

Reformation, there exists very considerable doubt as to what Luther thought that the Word of God prescribed, and this is where the controversy rages. It will be remembered that the Lutheran Churches came ultimately to be organized on Erastian lines as *Landeskirchen*. Rieker,[1] followed by Sohm,[2] expressed the view that Luther retained always in his thinking the medieval idea of the *Corpus Christianum*, mankind organized in a unitary society which operates both ecclesiastically and politically, and never seriously held the idea of a *Gemeinde* of Christians, separate from and independent of the State. Thus the actual development of the Lutheran Churches was in line with Luther's ideas of what the Word of God laid down. Troeltsch[3] accepts this view that the *Corpus Christianum* remained Luther's ideal, and carries it farther. He says that Luther expected the newly-founded *Gemeinden* to co-operate with the secular authorities and so work gradually outwards into universality; this was his method of reform. But events did not move in the hoped-for direction, and Luther expected therefore the speedy end of the world; the function of the *Gemeinden* came merely to be that of awaiting the end in Christian fellowship. But the *Landesherren* did in due course take up the idea of organizing reformed Churches themselves in their various dominions, with the result that the *Gemeinden* lost their reason for existence and Luther's original idea was realized in a modified form. Hermelink[4] thinks that the imminent prospect of the world's end prevented Luther from attaching much importance to the question of Church government, and does not ascribe the ideal of the *Corpus Christianum* to Luther. But he says that Luther never recognized any opposition between the Church and the State. His view was, according to Hermelink, that in normal times the clergy should be appointed by the spiritual power; if it failed, the secular authority should perform this task; if it failed to do so, and as a last resort, but only as a last resort, then each individual *Gemeinde* should appoint its own pastors and preachers. But the *Landesherr* was always to be regarded as representing and embodying the *Gemeinde*; the latter possessed, it is true, the ideal right, but in practice, except in an emergency, the *Landesherr*

---

[1] In *Die rechtliche Stellung der evangelischen Kirche Deutschlands*. (Owing to the war, it is impossible to check references to some German books.)

[2] In *Kirchenrecht*, I, 460–82.

[3] In *Protestantism and Progress* (English translation), Chs. II and III.

[4] In '*Zu Luthers Gedanken über Idealgemeinden und von weltlicher Obrigkeit*' (*Zeitschrift für Kirchengeschichte*, 29, 1908), and in a *Nachwort* to this, answering Drews (quoted on p. 49), in the same number of the same periodical.

should take any necessary steps, acting as its representative; and
even if he were not a Christian, the *Gemeinde* should not necessarily
take matters into its own hands. There was thus a natural
harmony between the *Gemeinde* and its *Landesherr*, and Luther's
idea of the Visitation of 1526 was that the *Gemeinde* and the *Landesherr* should work together in it. It follows that the final settlement
of Lutheranism was, except in certain details, a natural development of Luther's ideas concerning Church government.

Drews, on the other hand, answers his own question, 'Did the
State Church correspond to the Ideal of Luther?' with a decided
negative.[1] Luther, he holds, assumed, when he wrote the *an den
christlichen Adel*, that all the nobles were Christians, and called on
them in the existing emergency to do what all Christians had the
right to do, but the nobles had also the power to do, that is, to set
up a German Church which should be free of Rome, and in which
each *Gemeinde* would appoint its own pastors and preachers. But
the nobles disappointed him, and he came to believe that God
would carry out the reform without human aid, by building up a
national Church on the basis of the *Gemeinden*, each of them possessing full powers. This hope was not realized, but it was never
abandoned by Luther, who accepted *Staatskirchentum* in practice,
but never in theory. Holl[2] also gives a negative answer to Drews's
question, but arrives at it by a somewhat different route. In the
an den christlichen Adel, he says, Luther calls on the nobles as
Christians (not necessarily to a man), as an important branch of
the Church, and as qualified to represent the Church (since they
are entrusted by God with the maintenance of the divine ordering
of the world), to see that a Council is summoned, but he does not
call on them actually to carry out the suitable reforms, which are
the business of the spiritual authority—that is, the Council when
called. The nobles failed to respond, and so Luther relied on the
Gemeinden by themselves, unassisted by their *Landesherren*, until
the year 1525. But even while he was attaching so many hopes to
the *Gemeinden* he was also hoping to set up a *Volkskirche*, which was
the other strain in his thought about the Church. In 1525 he
seemed to see in the prospect of the Visitation the chance of setting
this up; at first he asked the nobles to look only into material
matters, but afterwards he extended the request to include
spiritual matters as well, for, he argued, the nobles are Christians

---

[1] This question ('*Entsprach das Staatskirchentum dem Ideale Luthers?*') is the title of his
article in the *Zeitschrift für Theologie und Kirche*, 18, 1908.

[2] op. cit., pp. 326–80.

D

and can act as representatives of the *Gemeinde*, and are called upon
in the existing conditions to take upon themselves the duties of
'emergency bishops'.[1] But this view is in essentials the same as
that which underlies the *an den christlichen Adel*, and to it Luther
remained faithful. But events were too strong for him, and in due
course, contrary to his deepest convictions on the subject, the
Landesherren emerged as regulators of the Church, not as Christians
and representatives of the *Gemeinden*, but simply in virtue of their
position as *Landesherren*. This view is not dissimilar to Hermelink's,
although its final conclusion is different.[2]

The most important result of this controversy is that it has
brought to light a number of opposing tendencies in the mind of
Luther and revealed a real uncertainty in his thought. It will,
even if it is continued, never be brought to a final conclusion, for
the reason that it is impossible to arrange all Luther's conflicting
tendencies into a coherent system. Yet he would have claimed of
each of them that it was derived from the Word of God. This
shows clearly enough that though in principle Luther held that the
Church should be regulated by the Word of God, yet the actual
obscurity of the Word, even to Luther's own mind, caused the
principle to remain abstract. But this fact, even if known to
Luther, did not cause him to alter in the least respect his views on
the subject of the predominance of the Word. To him, both the
first *Gemeinden* of the Reformation and the eventual *Landeskirchen*
were ordained and instituted by the Word.

The Word of God is supreme and demands complete submission
in affairs of State also. Each member of the government and the
government as a whole ought to be subservient to it; every subject of the government must order his relation to the government
in accordance with the commands of the Word. There is no trace
in Luther of the modern view, or of the beginning of a transition
towards the modern view, that the State is autonomous, possessing authority over its subjects in virtue of the function which it
performs, subject to no interference or supervision except from
those whose interests it claims to preserve and further; he would
have regarded with horror the smallest move in the direction of
secularizing the State or any of its functions. The State, according

---

[1] *Notbischöfe*.

[2] See also (though it has not been possible to consult these authorities) W. Köhler
in *Deutsche Zeitschrift für Kirchenrecht* (1906), pp. 211 sqq.; A. Schultze, *Stadtgemeinde und
Reformation* (1918); Meinecke, '*Luther über christliches Gemeinwesen und christlichen Staat*'
in *Historische Zeitschrift*, Bd. 121, pp. 1 sqq. The question has regained importance in
recent German Church conflicts.

to him, was set up by God and is maintained in its position by
God,[1] and must, of course, obey the regulations set forth for it by
God; and God makes known His regulations in His Word.

The Church, as we have seen, was brought into existence by
the Word, which was God's instrument in the matter. This is not
true, in Luther's view, of the State. For the latter came into existence before the Word of God was promulgated, and therefore was
created by the direct act of God. This took place, according to
Luther's usual view, as a direct result of the Fall of Man, and
would not have taken place otherwise, for man in his primitive
state of paradisal innocence did not need any government: there
was no polity before sin came, nor was there any need for it.[2]
There are occasional traces of a different view, that even in Paradise it was necessary to have a government,[3] but this does not seem
to represent Luther's real thought in the matter, or to be so readily
compatible with his other political opinions. Thus created by
the act of God to deal with the situation engendered by human
sin, the State must be subordinate to the Word of God: 'God
wishes to have them [sc. the princes] subjected to his Word; they
are to hear it or meet with complete disaster. It is enough that
they should hold authority over all men; over God's Word they
are to hold none. For God's Word establishes them, and makes
them gods,[4] and places all things under them. Therefore they
should not be above that which installs them and establishes them,
but should be subject to it, and allow themselves to be directed,
punished and controlled by it.'[5] It is a little difficult to see how
the governments were able to subordinate themselves to and
govern according to the dictates of the Word of God before that
Word was available, i.e. before the time of the giving of the law
to Moses. But Luther would perhaps have solved this problem
by giving the answer suggested by Paul's words in Romans ii. 14,
15, viz., that the statecraft of Melchisedek was directed by the
'law written in his heart', which was for him the Word of God.
However this may be, it is certain that from Moses onwards the

---

[1] 'es kompt nicht aus menschlichem willen odder furnemen, sondern Gott selbs alle oberkeit
setzet und erhellt', W.A., XXX, Part 1, p. 192 (1530).

[2] W.A., XLII, 79 (1525); cf. 'wenn nicht bose leut weren, so durfft man keyner ubirkeytt',
W.A., XII, 329 (1523).

[3] e.g. in W.A., XLII, 62: 'septimo die mane videtur Adam audivisse Dominum mandantem
curam oeconomicam et politicam cum prohibitione pomi.'

[4] i.e., though the State as such was set up by God's direct act, particular governments are set up by God's Word.

[5] W.A., XXX, Part 1, pp. 195, 196 (1530).

obligation imposed on governments to obey the Word was absolute and inevitable. It is easy enough to see that Luther approved the form of government which he did approve, viz. the polity of the Holy Roman Empire and of its constituent states, especially the German ones, for reasons other than that they conformed exactly to the prescriptions of the Word of God; but he would himself have bitterly repudiated this suggestion and claimed that the Word of God unmistakably laid down the political principles in question.

The principal, and in fact almost the only, duty of the subject in relation to the government is, according to Luther, to obey it. This obligation follows naturally and inevitably from the fact that the State is divinely ordained, and, strictly, no instruction from the Word of God is needed for us to become aware of it. Luther does from time to time ground the obligation to obey the State and the sinfulness of rebellion against it on the divine character of its ordinance, as in the following passage: 'God wishes the civil power to be held in high and sovereign regard, and that a man should be obedient and subject to it as to God's representative, just as to God Himself, with fear and all honour. For whoever wishes to set himself against it, or to be disobedient to it, or to despise those whom God names with His own name and calls gods, causing His honour to reside in them—whoever despises them, is disobedient to them, or sets himself against them, that man despises the true and supreme God, who is in them and speaks and exercises rule through them, who calls their judgement His judgement.'[1] But his general custom is much more to urge that subjects must obey their legally constituted authority because the Word of God commands them to do so. This comes out clearly in the whole trend of the argument in the *von weltlicher Oberkeit*,[2] and especially in the part of that work in which he justifies the taking up of arms by a Christian in obedience to his government; and even more clearly in the wearisome frequency with which he quotes Romans xiii. 1–3 in all parts of his writings to prove immediately the duty of obedience to the State.[3] He says, too, that Christians derive their knowledge that the emperor is to be recognized as their lord and obeyed as such from the Holy Scripture.[4] Moreover, as we have seen above,[5] the government

---

[1] *W.A.*, XXX, Part 1, p. 192 (1530).   [2] *W.A.*, XI, 246–80 (1523).

[3] This text is apparently still regarded by modern German theologians (e.g. Karl Heim) as the only proper basis of a Christian political philosophy.

[4] *W.A.*, XXIX, 599 (1529).   [5] pp. 51, 52.

is required to direct its policy in accordance with the Word of
God, and the subject therefore when he obeys the government is
in effect obeying the prescriptions of the Word of God, mediated
to him by the government.

Although a subject may never and in no circumstances rebel
against his government—even if a bloodthirsty tyranny is established, all that he is to do is to busy himself yet more assiduously
than ever in carrying out his proper function in the community—
there is one occasion on which he is released from his obligation
of positive obedience to it. This occurs when the government
interferes with religious matters and seeks to impose a doctrine or
ceremonial by force on Christians; in such a case the subject
should simply refuse to obey, and take any painful consequences
which may ensue with courage, and in fact with joy.[1] Luther
proves this from Acts v. 29, 'We must obey God rather than men',
and says that if we suffer as a result of our disobedience we are
suffering 'for the sake of God's Word'. Thus even when a subject
disobeys his government, so long as he does so on right grounds, he
is still submitting to the Word of God. The obligation thus to
submit is one which he can never escape, and the Word of God is
thus the real controlling influence in his political life.[2]

We see, then, that in his personal life, both religious and secular,
in his family life, in his ecclesiastical life, and in his political life
each man must unreservedly and in every detail submit himself
wholly to the Word of God, to be found within the pages of the
Bible. There is only one consideration which forbids us to say
that a man is controlled by the Word of God at every moment of
his life from the cradle to the grave, and that is the merciful
proviso that we are allowed to do what is not expressly forbidden
in the Word.[3] We are thus entitled on the whole to eat, drink,
and dress as we like. But apart from this we are bound, regulated
and controlled by the Word of God, and all the intellectual and
moral freedom that we have is that involved by the right to spread
the Christian faith and live the Christian life, and to confute the
errors and reprove the sins of those who think and live differently.
It is, of course, completely true that Luther's intellectual and
moral life was not in practice so fettered and confined as his
theory demanded that it should be, and that the Reformation

[1] *W.A.*, XI, 266, 267 (*von weltlicher Oberkeit*, 1523).
[2] For a full account of Luther's political ideas see Kurt Matthes, *Luther und die Obrigkeit*.
[3] *W.A.*, XVIII, 110 (1525) (quoted above, p. 40).

started by him achieved a great liberation of the human spirit; but we are to ascribe these things to the inward awakening brought to pass by the direct contact with God of the souls of Luther and his disciples, not to the theory offered as an interpretation of this experience. The theory remains stark and inflexible.

We finally conclude, therefore, that Luther set up the totalitarian omnicompetent Word of God in place of the totalitarian, omnicompetent Church of the Middle Ages. He was able to free his soul from the trammels of legalistic religion, and his emancipation placed him outside the fold of the Catholic Church; but he could not free his mind from its craving for an external, objective authority. In other words, while he was religiously the precursor of the modern spirit, intellectually he remained in the Middle Ages. Melanchthon and more especially the Protestant Schoolmen have been often criticized for standardizing and petrifying Luther's living theology by relapsing into Biblicism; in reality they were following in their master's footsteps when they treated the content of faith as written and laid down once and for all; they differed from him merely in making the text of the Bible as a whole rather than the Word of God into the infallible repository of doctrine.

This view about Luther is to be distinguished from that of Troeltsch, who says, 'The hierarchical sacramental Church is replaced [*sc.* by Luther] by the Church which lays the main emphasis upon the Word of Scripture and its proclamation by the preachers',[1] after asserting that 'the Word itself, its foundation in the Bible, its manifestation in the Sacrament, and its proclamation in the sermon, is to him an objective and precious endowment'.[2] The whole of the supernatural element in the Church, says Troeltsch, is focused in the Word, but the Church is that which controls and orders the lives of all Christians.[3] Troeltsch is so far right, in that he recognizes that Luther was sufficiently medieval to be incapable of dispensing with an external, all-embracing authority. But he is too much concerned to fit Luther exactly into his universal classification of forms of Christianity into those belonging to the 'Church' type and those belonging to the 'sect' type, to give their proper weight to the numerous passages in which Luther places the Word high above the Church and his frequent disparagement of the latter, even in its reformed aspect,

---

[1] *Die Sociallehre der Christlichen Kirchen* (English translation), II, 478.
[2] ibid.   [3] ibid.

in favour of the former. The Church is not to Luther the divine institution which uses the preaching of the Word to convert the world and combine its members into the Christian fellowship; on the contrary, the Word uses the Church as the means by which it can be proclaimed to all the world. We cannot say that Luther belongs either to the 'Church' type, or to the 'sect' type; he resists this classification. But if we amend the Troeltschian classification to (a) those who require an external authority, and (b) those who insist on an inward authority, we can without qualification assign Luther to the former class.

III

Will Luther's answer to the problem of authority hold? It has one great merit. It genuinely seeks to objectivize the content of religious faith. Every inward religion, and especially Christianity, has to be perpetually on its guard against a great and insidious danger—that of insisting so strongly on the essentially personal character of religious conviction and experience as to allow or cause people to suppose that their own inward experiences provide an adequate revelation of the whole content of faith, or even that it does not matter what they believe, so long as they have, or think that they have, the right experience. Only if it wards off this danger can it make good the claim which at least Christianity, by its very nature, implicitly makes, to provide an adequate explanation of and purpose for the whole of human life, social and individual; if it does not ward off this danger it sinks to the level of being merely a personal solace in time of trouble and a castle of retreat for the individual soul. It can ward off this danger in only one way, by providing an interpretation of the whole universe which is not only capable of meeting any amount of philosophical criticism, but is also in the full sense objective and absolute, i.e. independent of the historical or personal perspective of any individual, of the collapse or survival of any human institutions, of its acceptance by anyone, of the feelings produced by its acceptance or non-acceptance, and of the physical existence of the human race.

Luther's doctrine of authority does attempt to provide such an interpretation. It says: other than and independent of human speculations and reasonings stands the Word of God, once and for all spoken to man and written down, inerrant, beyond criticism, objective and absolute. Man may believe it or not as he wishes; its truth is not affected by man's attitude to it. It is not judged by man; rather, it judges man. Human science and philosophy may seek to discredit and supersede it, and may even claim to have done so; but that is only so much the worse for human science and philosophy. 'The grass withereth, the flower fadeth, but the Word of our God shall stand for ever.'

But unfortunately this attempt at objectivization fails. For what is this Word of God? We have seen that it is a selection made by Luther from the Bible, and that the principle of selection is: does this or that writing preach Christ or not? If it does, it is evangelic and apostolic and part of the Word of God; if not, it is none of these things. We note that there is no attempt, or practically no attempt, to answer the question whether a book is apostolic by discovering whether it was in fact written by an Apostle. The principle of selection is religious, and once the religious question in the matter is answered, all other questions are automatically answered at the same time. But if we use as a principle of selection, Does this preach Christ or not? we are assuming that we know what a book says when it does preach Christ. This assumption is harmless enough if by 'preaching Christ' is meant 'giving information about the life, death, resurrection, ascension and living presence of Christ', and this is what Luther professes to mean by the phrase. But closer investigation shows that what he really, though perhaps unconsciously, means by it is 'proclaiming the Pauline interpretation of the career of Christ'; this is shown, for instance, by his naïve view that the Epistle to the Romans preaches Christ better than any other book in the Bible. Thus we find that the 'Word of God' turns out to be in essence 'that which Paul preaches'—not even Christ, but Paul. And even this is not the worst aspect of the matter. We have seen that Luther's real reason for accepting Paul's theology was that it—or, rather, a certain part of it—had brought peace and confidence and the certainty of forgiveness to his troubled soul at a time of great agony and despair. This means that he accepted the Pauline theology and elevated it to the rank of a criterion for distinguishing the Word of God, partly because it mediated to him the experience of forgiveness, and partly because it gave him an interpretation of that experience which seemed to him to be true. Thus we are asked to accept such and such books as the Word of God because Luther's religious experience—not the religious experience of the whole of mankind, nor of the whole Christian Church, nor of the whole body of Lutheran Christians, but Luther's[1]—commended them to him as such. But it is clearly impossible to assert that a certain source of religious truth is objectively authoritative on the evidence of one person's subjective experience. In fact, instead of an objective religion we find a blank subjectivism, heavily, but not impenetrably, disguised.

But let us suppose that Luther has made good his claim that the Word of God as defined by him is objective and absolute. The Word of God, as we have it, and indeed as on this view God presumably intended us to have it, is written down in languages which are foreign to everyone who reads it, and were foreign to every reader in the time of Luther also. This is not perhaps an important fact as far as the scholar is concerned—opinions will differ as to exactly how important it is for him—but for the great mass of people, whose task it is to regulate their lives according to the prescriptions which the Word contains, a translation becomes imperative. Luther himself was, of course, among the very first to realize and satisfy this need. And every translation is a surreptitious exegesis. Thus most, in fact nearly all, Christians submit themselves, not to the Word of God, but to the Word of God as interpreted by some translator or other—as interpreted by Luther, if they are Lutherans. We are then faced by a dilemma: the great majority of Christians must either say that in theory they submit themselves to the Word of God, but that as they do not clearly know what that Word says they can make only provisional decisions on nearly all subjects, or they must submit to the Word of God as interpreted by someone more learned than themselves, e.g. Luther. The second alternative is invariably the one adopted in practice, but clearly introduces the element of subjectivism at a vital juncture.

But has the scholar, however learned, evangelical, and devout, direct access to the Word of God? Only if the meaning of the text of the Word is in its entirety clear and indubitable to all those who have the necessary degree of learning, evangelicalism, and devoutness. Luther certainly believed quite sincerely that it was, and his rigidly dogmatic attitude is logically as unanswerable as that of the man who asserts that he knows by immediate intuition that the world is flat like a pancake. But no one now agrees with Luther; and although this disagreement is greatly reinforced by modern criticism, Luther had no real excuse for taking up the attitude which he did take up even in his own time. For he was

---

[1] Of course, his experience was typical of many people's; and he may well have thought that his was a universal experience, as people often do about their experience.

faced, and knew perfectly well that he was faced, in his Biblical studies and in his controversies, by a formidable array of variant interpretations of practically every important passage in the Bible, and of a great number of unimportant passages as well. He was led to the unshakeable conviction that his interpretation was the correct one by his experience of justification by faith, and we may agree that his exegesis of the passages relating to this particular subject, and indeed many others, is as good and illuminating as any that has ever been produced; but this experience did not invest him with infallible insight into the meaning of the entire Word of God. The meaning of the Word of God is in many passages doubtful, and even the scholar with the best qualifications is on the horns of much the same dilemma as we have seen the great mass of Christians to be: either he must admit that he does not know the meaning of the Word of God, and therefore cannot act with conviction, and his submission to the Word of God comes to be purely theoretical, or else he submits to one interpretation of the Word (his own or someone else's) rather than another, and is plunged into the depths of subjectivism. Protestant divines have on the whole adopted the latter alternative, and Luther himself did so.

The objections which we have so far raised to Luther's doctrine of authority might have been, and in point of fact often were, raised by Luther's opponents in his own and immediately subsequent times. There are other objections which could not have occurred to any of his contemporaries or their immediate successors, and are made possible only by modern trends of thought. They do not therefore touch Luther himself or discredit his thinking, since they could scarcely have been avoided or countered by him. But they deserve to be mentioned, if only because in the hands of several recent exponents of Continental neo-Lutheran theology the renewed emphasis on the *Wort Gottes* emerges as a virtual return to the Lutheran conception of the Word of God and its authority.[1]

The first of these objections is this: Luther's conception of certain books in the Bible as God's final Word to man, directing him once and for all as to the right way of conducting his personal and social life, makes certain assumptions about the nature of God's revelation to man and human knowledge in general which it is necessary to reject. Luther assumes that a body of knowledge,

---

[1] This is true of K. Heim. Is it not also partly true of Barth, whose views are, however, developed much more directly from Calvin's than from Luther's?

adequate to the whole needs of man in every age and representing all the knowledge which the limitations of the human mind enabled it to acquire, was imparted by God many centuries ago to a number of men, nearly all (perhaps all) belonging to the Jewish race and living within certain definite limits of time. But the history of human knowledge, in religion as well as in other matters, has convinced us that God imparts knowledge gradually and steadily as the human mind is able to understand and assimilate it, and that this remains true even when due allowance has been made for the occasional emergence of geniuses in religion and other branches of life, men and women who have been able to see far beyond the limits of their own age and place and race. The prophets and Apostles were, despite their greatness, limited; God, therefore, did not tell them all that there was to know. We observe consequently within the Bible itself very distinct traces of a progressive revelation; we are compelled to expect to find, and believe that we do find, just as distinct traces of the continuance of that progressive revelation beyond the pages of the Bible down to the present day. If this is so, we cannot claim to find in the Bible a definitive, once-and-for-all revelation of God's mind and purposes to man. The Bible possesses great authority in the broad and non-technical sense of that word; it does not possess authority in the strictest sense of the word.

The second objection from the modern point of view is this: we have praised Luther for his attempt at making the content of religious faith objective. But it is very doubtful whether this can ever be done by erecting a purely external authority and submitting to it, however venerable and reliable it may be; by 'a purely external authority' is meant an authority which after the initial act of personal submission expresses its decrees and dogmas from a position entirely outside the individual. Such an authority is unsatisfactory because when a man makes his initial submission to it he cannot know more than that it is in general trustworthy and accurate; he cannot know that all its future judgements will be correct; and once he has submitted and the authority becomes external to him he has no power of testing these judgements. But unless he does know that its future as well as its past judgements are to be trusted he has no good reason for submitting at all. If, of course, he does know that they are to be trusted or leaves himself with the means of finding out whether they are or not, the authority ceases to be purely external. If all this is so, the attempt to make the content of faith objective by appointing an external authority is vitiated by an unacknowledged gap in the argument.

Luther set up a purely external authority in the form of the Word of God. It was not purely external as far as he personally was concerned. His own full submission to the Word of God took place as a result of his experience of justification, which, as he held, had been mediated to him by the Word of God; but at the time of his submission his knowledge of the Scriptures was large enough for him to be able to justify his submission on the grounds of its established accuracy and consistency; and, what is far more important, his submission did not mean the abnegation of the right to investigate and even to criticize the Scriptures, as is shown by the mental processes which led to the distinction between the Scriptures and the Word of God, and by his writings about the books of the Bible before and after that distinction had been made. In other words, Luther himself maintained living contact with his source of authoritative teaching, and in his submission to it there was always present the element of active personal agreement with what it had to say. But for Luther's followers the case was necessarily different. They could not be, and were not, expected to do anything more than submit to the Word of God, and its authority for them was bound to be purely external. Luther and his successors could have avoided the force of this objection by encouraging and producing in all Lutherans that active co-operation with the Word of God which their founder possessed. But we do not find any trace of their having done so, and, as a matter of history, the whole tendency in the post-Lutheran age was much more in the direction of making the authority of the Word even more external than Luther had left it.

These arguments, which lead us to reject the Lutheran idea of authority as inadequate and untrue, do not involve the further view that the whole concept of the authoritative Word of God is worthless. We renounce the suggestion that the Word is identical with certain selected writings, that it has spoken once and for all, that its authority is purely external. We have met no reason for refusing to believe that there is a Word of God, i.e. that there is an absolute and objective truth, revealed wholly or partially by God to men. If there is a Word of God in this sense, it is presumably authoritative. But we have yet to find this Word of God, and we have seen reason to believe that when it is found its authority will be internal as well as external, i.e. that it will demand no blind submission, but the continued active, personal co-operation of each individual, manifesting itself in renewed acts of intelligent, reasoned acceptance. Did the other Reformers succeed in finding the Word of God, or other source of authoritative teaching, and did they discover what was the right kind of authority to ascribe to it? Luther has not provided us with an answer to our fundamental problem, but he has, by asserting that there is a Word of God, given us an inkling of the way in which it may perhaps be discovered.

CHAPTER II

ZWINGLI

I

To what extent, if at all, and in what sense did Zwingli recognize the problem of authority? When we turn from Luther to Zwingli, we move into a very different atmosphere. The external conditions under which the two men had to work were in many respects similar enough: the entrenched religious and semi-political supremacy of the Papal hierarchy, the vague stirrings towards spiritual liberty in the minds of many men of insight and piety, nationalistic aspirations and resentment of foreign influence in finance and politics obscurely formulating themselves among the mass of ordinary people, critical and aesthetic discoveries disintegrating within cultivated minds the fabric of medieval polity and metaphysics. The conflicts, too, which the two men undertook, followed not wholly dissimilar courses and led to not wholly dissimilar results: in each case the hopes and dreams and ambitions and prayers of many different classes of people became incarnate in one prophetic personality who regarded himself as charged with a divine commission; in each case this one personality, armed with mingled divine and human strength, made his onslaught against positions embattled by age-long tradition, comprehensive authority claimed and conceded, the dominion of the systematic intellect, and deep-rooted popular piety; in each case, after a comparatively short struggle, he established himself as the representative of a power which had for the future to be reckoned among those which shaped the destiny of Europe.

But the personalities in which the conflicts centred were of a widely divergent type. The dynamic of Luther was emotional, not intellectual: the function which he ascribed to his mind was that of interpreting and enunciating an experience which entered his life by the door of the emotions, and of drawing out its implications for ecclesiastical and social life. We can see this clearly when we reflect that the evangelical experience of Luther was, in the age in which he lived, revolutionary in its implications for the life of the mind and the spirit, but that Luther himself drew out very few of these implications and remained encased intellectually within the framework of medieval thought. But exactly the opposite was true of Zwingli. He attained his far-reaching ideas almost exclusively by intellectual reflection, and worked them out ruthlessly to their logical conclusion; his emotions became the servants of his intellect, and supplied the driving force which enabled him to put into practical effect, in the teeth of all opposition, the conclusions which his thought had reached. But that the force of intellectual fervour is at least as great as that of emotional fervour receives some measure of proof from the fact that Zwingli died fighting on the field of battle for the realization in practical politics of his intellectual convictions.

Zwingli's youth and early manhood were untroubled by religious difficulties, or doubts as to the truth of orthodox dogma. In fact, there is very little reason for supposing that he was at all interested in religion, except in a purely conventional way. At the age of fourteen he went to live in Berne and to be educated there by Wölflin, known principally as a humanist, and as very fond of music, but also as a reformer in his later years in the city in which he taught. Wölflin's influence on Zwingli seems to have been of a purely academic nature; but it meant that Zwingli learnt from him an enthusiasm for humanistic studies which never deserted him and became increasingly important in his total development. In 1500, now sixteen years of age, Zwingli proceeded to the University of Vienna, where he lived a jolly life of humanistic studies and ordinary pleasures. This continued when, two years later, he went to the University of Basel, to continue his work for a degree and support himself by teaching in the school of St. Martin's Church. Here he remained until 1506, and in his last year attended the lectures of the humanist, Thomas Wyttenbach, together with several men who also became famous in later years as reformers, including Capito, Pellicanus, and Leo Judaeus. Wyttenbach induced him for the first time to take an interest in religious problems, and in particular taught him a lesson which Luther was to teach the world in much more dramatic fashion twelve years later—that indulgences were a snare and an illusion, since the death of Christ alone was the price for the remission of sins. Zwingli paid tribute at least twice in later years to this contribution of Wyttenbach to his thought: in his *Expositio Articulorum* (the Sixty-seven Articles promulgated by him in 1523 as a preparation for the First Disputation at Zürich, held in that year) he says that in 1519 he did not learn much from Luther's views on indulgences; 'For I had learned previously about indulgences, that they were a deceit and a fable, from a disputation conducted some time ago at Basel by Doctor Thomas Wyttenbach of Briel, albeit in my absence'.[1] He repeats this tribute in a paper addressed to Luther in 1527.[2]

But, despite the influence on him in this respect of Wyttenbach, and his recognition of its value, at least later on, Zwingli continued without difficulty to accept and preach the orthodoxy of his time for several years, becoming parish priest of Glarus in 1506 and remaining intellectually undisturbed until at least 1514. We are to imagine him as entering the ranks of the clergy because it was a normal and natural thing for a man of his education to do, and not because of any particular sense of vocation to it, and as carrying out the duties involved neither with excessive enthusiasm nor with culpable laxity. But although there is no hint of revolt against current beliefs or even of mental tumult on their account, we can scarcely suppose that Zwingli's acute mind was not actively engaged in reflection on the dogmas which it was his business to teach and preach. No doubt, then, it was as the climax of a long process of thought that two events occurred in the years 1514 and 1515 (we cannot fix more precisely the date of either of them) which were of decisive importance for the future development of Zwingli's mind. The first was the beginning of a profound interest in and admiration for the writings and ideas of Erasmus. He describes this for us in the *Expositio Articulorum* of 1523 in the following words: 'Eight or nine years ago I read a poem full of comfort by the very learned Erasmus of Rotterdam, written to the Lord Jesus in very noble language, in which Jesus complains that men do not seek all good from him, although he is the Source of all Good, the Saviour, comfort and treasure of the soul'.[3] Apart from the importance of this occurrence in the development of Zwingli's views about the all-sufficiency of Christ for salvation, and about 'reformed' notions generally, we must notice that it has a further importance of especial relevance to our subject. For it led to the immersion of Zwingli in the writings of Erasmus and his sharing in the latter's enthusiasm for the Scriptures. Erasmus, we know, moreover, was strongly in favour of bringing Christian beliefs and practices to the touchstone of Scripture, though without elevating his respect for Scripture into a dogma, and we must imagine Zwingli, in view of what followed, as being strongly influenced by that element in the thought of

---

[1] *Zwinglis Werke* in the *Corpus Reformatorum* (to which all Zwinglian references in future apply), II, 145. (Kidd, *Documents of the Continental Reformation*, gives the passage in its Latin translation in No. 159, p. 377.)

[2] V, 718.   [3] II, 217.

Erasmus. At any rate it cannot be rash to assert that the other important event of these years, 1514–15, was not entirely unconnected with the one that we have just described. This event also is described for us by Zwingli himself, both in the *Apologeticus Archeteles* of 1522 and in the *von der Klarheit und Gewissheit oder Untrüglichkeit des Wortes Gottes* of the same year. In the *Archeteles* he says: 'While I was diligently considering these matters [*sc.*, whether one should believe the writings of the philosophers or the Scriptures as to the right method of acquiring eternal felicity], and praying to God to show me the answer to my doubt, God said to me: Why, O foolish one, do you not think thus: "the truth of the Lord abides for ever, and thou art to keep close to that truth"; and "the heaven and the earth will pass away, but my words will not pass away; the things of men shall be destroyed, but the things of God are unchangeable"; and "in vain do they worship me, teaching the doctrines and commands of men, as if God ought to obey our counsels, and as if, when we have discovered something which seems at first sight beautiful, honourable and even holy, that would at once please God; instead of supposing that we must rather see to it that we depend with all our hearts on him, and not on our own resolutions and discoveries".'[1] In the *von der Klarheit und Gewissheit usw.*, presumably referring to the same occurrence, he says: ' . . . I know for certain that God teaches me, for I have experienced[2] it: but do not wilfully misinterpret the word; you must understand how I know that God teaches me: I made as good progress in my youth in human learning as many of my age, and when seven or eight years ago I applied myself to the Holy Scriptures, the philosophy and theology of the wranglers were always anxious to object. But I finally came to the point where I thought—led to it, of course, by the Scripture and God's Word—: "you must leave all these things on one side and learn God's meaning simply from his own simple Word." '[3]

It should be noted that the experience just described in Zwingli's own words was a genuinely religious experience. The view is sometimes expressed that because Zwingli arrived at his conclusions by intellectual means he is to be regarded, not as a religious, but as an intellectual leader. In accordance with this, Lindsay puts him on a lower level than Luther and Calvin because of his 'clerical marriage' with Anna Reinhard, which was legalized only in 1525, and because he finds no trace of personal religion until the death of his brother in 1520.[4] But it is fairly

[1] I, 260.   [2] *empfunden.*   [3] I, 379.   [4] *History of the Reformation*, II, 38.

E

certain that the feeling in regard to 'clerical marriages' was quite
different in the sixteenth century from what a similar institution
would arouse in our own day, and Zwingli thought of it much
more as an illustration of the foolishness of Papal regulations than
as an example of moral turpitude or indeed as a moral or religious
question at all. And the plain inference to be drawn from the
Zwinglian passages just quoted is that Zwingli is describing the
direct answer of God to his spirit when he was in trouble and
doubt and was seeking through prayer to obtain divine assistance. It is true that the answer came to him through the medium
of his intellect, but it is false to erect an antithesis between intellectual and religious experience; neither excludes the other.

The birth and growth of his admiration for Erasmus, and his
discovery that truth must be found in the Scriptures alone, virtually settled the future course of his career. Of course, their implications did not immediately and without hindrance dominate
all his thinking and acting. The years 1516–18, during which he
was People's Priest at Einsiedeln, were years in which he studied
the Scriptures with great care and gradually worked out the consequences of the light which had dawned upon him. Thus, on
the one hand, throughout his stay at Einsiedeln his sermons on
the Gospels preached at Mass relied much upon the exegesis
provided by the Fathers, and as late as September, 1518, he
accepted the post of Acolyte Chaplain to the Pope; on the other
hand, he told the Cardinal of Sitten that the claims of the Papacy
were based on an insecure foundation and could not be supported
from Scripture, and wrote several letters in frank criticism of the
pardoner Bernhardin Samson. Zwingli himself in several places
indicates that the end of the year 1516 marked the beginning of
his evangelical preaching,[1] and it is clear that these apparent
vacillations were due to the fact that he was feeling his way towards a fully thought-out and articulated position. It is true that
his attacks on Samson were couched in the terms of intellectual
mockery and were deduced from humanist presuppositions. But
we may not therefore conclude that they were merely intellectual
exercises betraying no real concern for the interests of Christ and
His Church, as Lindsay appears to do when he says that they did
not reach the depths of religious feeling, and contrasts them un-
favourably in this respect with Luther's onslaught on Indulgences.[2]
It is impossible to separate the humanist from the religious man
within the personality of Zwingli, for he was at all times both a

[1] e.g. in the *Archeteles, ad init.*, I, 256.   [2] op. cit., II, 30.

humanist and a Christian; and it is in any case by no means desirable to do so.

The climax of this period of reflection roughly coincided with its conclusion. At the end of 1518 Zwingli was appointed People's Priest at Zürich, and entered upon that office at the beginning of 1519; he at once announced his intention of preaching on the Gospel of Matthew without reference to the Fathers or any human assistance whatever.[1] This announcement and its carrying out probably mark a definite break with the past and the intention of diverting his activities into the channels of positive reform. This view cannot be proved, but the repudiation of the Papal pension, the persuasion of the Town Council that all preaching must be Biblical, the public eating of meat in Lent and eventually the measures which constitute the Reformation in Zürich all follow naturally upon this event. Moreover, it is natural that his transference to a new sphere of activity, as being an obvious opportunity for the striking out of a new path, should stimulate him to a final decision on the question of his relation to the 'reformed' ideas with which he had now become thoroughly acquainted. There is, besides, no further sign of vacillation, real or apparent, after his arrival in Zürich. But even if the time of his final decision did not exactly coincide with that arrival, it followed it at no great distance. It should be noticed here that Zwingli was very careful in later years to deny that his 'reformed' activities were undertaken because he was a follower of Luther; rather, he asserts, both Luther (whose writings he scarcely knew) and he were followers of Christ who obeyed the commands of the Word of God.[2]

We need not follow Zwingli's career any farther in detail, since we already have enough material for answering the question set at the beginning of this section. We can observe at once that, as soon as Zwingli became interested in religious problems or perceived that there were religious problems of importance at all, one of the two problems that presented itself to him was concerned with authority. Which is to be trusted, he asked himself, the writings of philosophers or the Word of God? It is fairly clear that if the question is thus put, it admits of only one answer, especially for anyone who has put it in that way; God certainly knows more than men. But Zwingli did put it in this way, without being aware that he was at the same time virtually begging it; and came, of course, to the inevitable answer. Zwingli also tells

[1] II, 145.   [2] II, 145 sqq.

us how the issue was decided for him—by the voice of God,
speaking to him directly. From the way in which he speaks of this
experience afterwards, it is clear that he regarded the question
and its answer, at the time and afterwards, as being of fundamental
importance, more important, probably, than the question of the
mediatorial sufficiency of Christ, which was exercising his mind
at the same time. Having formulated the question and received
its answer, he looked at all other questions from that time forward
in the light of that answer, testing all doctrines and all practices
by their conformity to the Word of God, and criticizing all
opponents on the score of their failure to be true to the Word
of God.

We conclude, therefore, that from 1514–15 onwards Zwingli
recognized the problem of authority, and recognized it as being
of supreme importance; and we may add, on the basis of our
evidence, that he put it and answered it in an intellectual, although not therefore not religious, form: what is the absolutely
trustworthy source of truth, philosophical speculation embodied
in the decrees of the Roman Church, or the Bible?

II

What was Zwingli's answer to the problem of authority? It is
not necessary to prove at length that the Word of God occupied
the place of supreme authority in Zwingli's mind at the beginning
of his work in Zürich; that is sufficiently obvious from what has
already been said. We must, however, before amplifying his view,
establish the answer to the question whether Zwingli remained
faithful to it throughout the rest of his life. In the *Apologeticus
Archeteles* of August 1522, Zwingli complains of the Bishop of
Constance's action in sending a Commission to deal with affairs
in Zürich: 'How much more proper would it have been, if I had
taught anything contrary to true religion, to join issue openly with
me, and to show by the Scripture's[1] authority, naming me
openly,[2] where I had sinned and what sins I had committed.'
But he says that he will not object to the Commission's proceedings, 'so long as they allow the sacred writings to be the sacred
anchor, in which not to have trust is the greatest treachery and
impiety'.[3] In the *von der Klarheit und Gewissheit usw.* of the same

---

[1] It is already clear from the passages quoted that the Word of God stands in close
relation to the Scripture in Zwingli's mind. It is necessary to ask the reader to take
it for granted that the terms can be used interchangeably, and to prove this later on.

[2] *nominatim.*   [3] I, 259.

year, he says: 'The Word of God ought to be held by us in the highest honour—and by the "Word of God" understand only that which comes from the Spirit of God—and such faith given to no word as to it. For the Word of God is certain and cannot fail; it is bright and does not let man err in darkness; it teaches of itself, it makes itself plain, and illumines the human soul with all salvation and grace. . . .'[1] In 1523 he put right at the beginning of his Sixty-seven Articles, propounded by way of preparation for the First Public Disputation, this statement: 'All who say that the Gospel is nothing without the Church's guarantee, err and insult God',[2] and remarks in the Exposition of this Article that he has put it first with the express purpose that the opponents of the Gospel should be compelled to argue with him from the Bible without the aid of human teaching.[3] He then goes on, in this latter passage, to establish the article by passages from Scripture, which of course begs the question, but shows how central to him the idea of the supreme authority of the Word is.[4] Throughout the Articles and their Expositions, indeed, it is very plain that when he is not proving the authority of the Word he is taking it for granted, and that he regards a scriptural proof as in all cases decisive. In strict accordance with this, at the Disputation itself Zwingli answered the Bishop of Constance's first speech by asserting that it was not the business of the assembly to discuss the longevity of a custom, but whether it was commanded by God's law, and maintained throughout that the only argument which could be accepted was one from Scripture.[5] He stood firmly on the same ground at the Second Disputation, later in the same year.[6] We find him in 1525, in the Introduction to his *de vera et falsa Religione Commentarius*, saying: 'It is therefore very easy for us to write about the true and false religion of Christians, and give, as it were, an account of our faith which we have derived not from the stagnant pools of human wisdom, but from the rain of the Divine Spirit, which is the Word of God.'[7] The Baptists persistently asserted throughout their long controversy with Zwingli that they were carrying Zwingli's reliance on the Bible to its logical conclusion. In answer to them, for instance in the *von dem Touff, vom Widertouff, und vom Kindertouff* of May 1525, Zwingli made no attempt to retract his Biblicist position; on the contrary, he asserted that it was he who was faithful to the Scripture, and the Baptists who betrayed it, and set out to prove

---

[1] I, 382.   [2] I, 458.   [3] II, 21.   [4] II, 22 sqq.

[5] I, 479-569.   [6] II, 671-803.   [7] III, 639.

his position at length from the Scriptures.[1] In 1526, invited to a
Disputation at Baden, Zwingli laid down seven conditions for a
proper disputation, of which the first was that no other writing
than Holy Writ should be adduced, and the third that no judge
should be set over the Word of God: 'For the Word of God should
be our guide, by which we take our direction, and we ought not
to force it as we wish with our judgement . . . God's Word must
also direct and master our understandings, our meaning and our
art, and we must not make vain the Word of God.'[2] In the
writings of his later years Zwingli remained true to his position in
this matter; at Marburg he refused to admit to Luther that he had
shifted from his belief in the supreme authority of the Word of
God, and insisted that the difference between him and Luther was
one of the interpretation of Scripture. Finally, in the *Fidei Ratio*,
written and presented to the Emperor in 1530, Zwingli assumes
that the Christian creed is derived from the Word of God, and
has no standing except in so far as it accords therewith.[3] Thus
Zwingli remained faithful to his belief in the supremacy of
the Word.

A first reading of any of the writings of Zwingli already quoted
makes it clear at once that in his mind the Word of God stood in
very close relationship with the Scriptures. We cannot go farther
without determining what that relationship precisely was. The
locus classicus on the point must be the *von der Klarheit und Gewissheit des Wortes Gottes* of 1522.[4] This work at first sight places us in
a difficulty. After certain preliminary considerations, designed to
show that the 'inner man', being in the image of God, is gladdened
by nothing so much as the Word of God, the author proceeds to
treat its 'Certainty or Power'[5] (this is the title which he himself
gives to the section, and it is in fact impossible to see any difference
in his usage here between the meaning of the two words, and
'Certainty' is here used in the sense of 'Power'). Under this head
he quotes many instances from Scripture to prove that the Word
of God is always fulfilled, e.g. at the Creation God spoke, and His
Word created the universe from nothing. The Gospel itself, he
says, is an instance of the fulfilment of the Word of God. But here
the Word of God is plainly the directly spoken Word. Then he

---

[1] IV, 206 sqq.

[2] V, 12, 13 (*Eine freundliche Schrift an die Eidgenossen der 12 Orten usw.*).

[3] The volume in the *Corpus Reformatorum* containing this work has not yet appeared.
For extracts, *vide* Kidd, *Documents of the Continental Reformation*, No. 225.

[4] I, 338–84.   [5] *Gewissheit oder Kraft.*

turns to the 'Clarity'[1] of the Word. He begins this section by answering those who have suggested that the Word is by no means clear, because of the 'similes' and 'riddles'[2] that abound in it. These people obviously mean Scripture by the Word, and Zwingli obviously understands them to mean this. He answers them by many examples from Old and New Testaments in which God spoke to men and they immediately understood what He meant despite the contrariness of the message to the promptings of human reason. We are by now tempted to suppose that by the Word of God Zwingli means two things equally, the direct Word spoken to the individual soul, and Holy Writ, since this is the only interpretation that makes his argument logical. If this view is correct we are left with a very vague and loosely con-structed Word of God, and must ascribe to Zwingli a belief in something which later came to be known as the Inner Light. This interpretation of Zwingli's thought is supported by a passage in the 'Expositions' of the 67 Articles. In explanation of Article 1 he is concerned to prove that the authority of the Word is inde-pendent of the Church; he does so by means of numerous Scrip-tural quotations of cases in which the direct Word of God was thus independent, e.g. the voice of Christ to Paul on the Damascus road. If the Word of God is in his mind limited to the Bible, he has, of course, begged the question by endeavouring to prove its independence from passages contained within it; the logical fallacy is not so blatant if he includes in the Word of God the Word spoken to the individual soul, although it is still present. More importantly, what his arguments prove, if they prove any-thing, is the independence of the direct Word of God, not in any sense of the Bible.[3]

Yet there are almost innumerable passages in which Zwingli uses the 'Scripture' and the 'Word of God' as interchangeable terms, and there is not the slightest reason for supposing that under the term 'Scripture' is included anything not contained within the Bible. Moreover, Zwingli's protestation at the First Disputation, 'We have the inerrant and impartial judge, to wit, the divine Scripture, which cannot lie or deceive',[4] is robbed of much of its point if Zwingli was really ready to admit as 'judge' in cases of theological dispute the direct Word of God spoken since the writing of the Bible. Similarly, the conditions laid down by him for the projected disputation at Baden in 1526[5] lose much of their

---

[1] Klarheit. [2] Gleichnisse; Rätsel. [3] II, 22–7.
[4] I, 498. [5] Quoted, supra, p. 70.

force on this hypothesis. Moreover, there is no passage in Zwingli in which he distinguishes, as Luther does, the Word of God from the Scripture. There is no passage, it is true, either, in which he explicitly identifies the Word of God with the Scripture. But numerous passages do imply that to him they were in fact identical. In the *von der Klarheit und Gewissheit des Wortes Gottes*, while still attempting to prove that the Word of God is clear, he says: 'Hear, you wranglers, who refuse your faith to the Scripture, that the Word of God, which is God himself, illumines all men.'[1] Here, surely, he implies that what is true of one is true of the other. Towards the end of the work, after a long passage asserting the insusceptibility of the Scripture to human testing and adjudication, in which he says, for instance, 'The Scripture has come from God, not men',[2] he sums up what he has said by concluding: 'The Word of God ought to be held by us in the highest honour—and by "the Word of God" understand only that which comes from the Spirit of God—and such faith given to it as to no other word.'[3] Surely here too he is virtually asserting of the Word of God what he has previously proved to be true of the Scripture, without thinking it necessary to give further argument. There are many other passages which include, to a greater or less degree, the same implication, from which we may select the following strong example: in the *Auslegung* of the Fifteenth Article, Zwingli says (what he is frequently saying) that he will submit to having no human adjudicator of the Scripture, since only the Scripture is true; then he quotes John viii. 31, 'if ye abide in my word then are ye truly my disciples', and concludes: 'We have shown clearly enough that a man learns the Word and meaning of God not from men, but from the one Spirit of God. . . . See, my dear brothers, the certainty of the Word of God does not come from the judgement of men, but from God. . . .'[4] And in general, it may be asserted that the identification of the Scripture with the Word of God fits in with all the passages in which Zwingli discusses the one or the other, with the important exception of those passages mentioned at the beginning of the treatment of this point.

These require some explanation if we are about to accept the identification. Two suggestions may be made. The first is that the difficulty which they create arises from a confusion inside Zwingli's mind. Let us suppose that the Scripture and the Word of God meant exactly the same thing to him; he was called upon to prove the 'Power', and later the 'Clarity' of the Word of God,

[1] I, 365.   [2] I, 382.   [3] ibid. (quoted on p. 69, *supra*).   [4] II, 75.

or the Scripture. His mind travelled to another meaning which the Word of God, in a non-technical sense, could obviously bear, the Word actually and directly spoken by God to men; the confusion is assisted by the fact that the examples of this that he has in mind are described in the Scripture. The confusion, which had occurred in this way in the *von der Klarheit und Gewissheit usw.*, recurred in his mind when he was writing the Exposition of Article 1.

The second suggestion[1] is that the confusion was partly due also to an idea which Zwingli very probably held, although he nowhere states it explicitly: that the Bible is not simply the record of God's dealings with and words to the Jews, the early Christians, and mankind in general, but also the means by which He speaks directly and personally to the condition of every individual who wishes Him to speak in that way. This belief underlies Augustine's account of his conversion and is very much to the fore in the evangelical experience of Luther: Zwingli may be said to imply it in his account of his own conversion[2] and in the passages on personal religious experience which we shall later be considering.[3] If it *was* in his mind when he thought of the Word of God, it is very likely that the distinction between the Word of God to the individual mediated by the Bible and the Word of God coming to him directly would become blurred.

If one of these explanations, or something like it, is correct, we are entitled to conclude that Zwingli identified the Word of God with the Scripture; and in default of any reference to them, we may further say that he obliterated the useful and time-honoured distinctions between the value and purpose of the Law and the Gospel, and between the Old Testament and the New Testament. We can in future therefore imitate without danger Zwingli's own custom of using the Scripture and the Word of God as interchangeable terms.

We are now at last in a position to examine in detail what supremacy it was that Zwingli assigned to the Word of God, or the Bible. We know that it was for the individual the authoritative source of religious truth. From the point of view of the times in which he lived and the particular conflict to which his energies were devoted his most important further assertion on the subject is that the Word of God is independent of the Church. In 1522 the Bishop of Constance sent, together with his Commission for

---

[1] I owe this to some comments by Mr. C. G. Stone.
[2] *vide* p. 65, *supra*.   [3] *vide* pp. 87, 88, *infra*.

setting in order the affairs of Zürich, a *Paraenesis* addressed to the
Senate. Zwingli deals with this document point by point in his
Apologeticus Archeteles. In his thirty-sixth section, the Bishop
virtually says that the Gospel is dependent on the unity of the
Church.[1] Zwingli answers this statement at length. It should be
noted first of all that in Zwingli's writings the word 'Gospel' is as
interchangeable with 'Word of God' and 'Scripture' as they are
with one another.[2] 'Surely there was in existence the Gospel in
the times of Arius, when the Church was split from top to bottom?'
he asks. After answering possible objections to this argument, he
goes on to extend the range of the discussion by referring to
Augustine's famous saying: 'I should not believe the Gospel, if the
Church had not approved the Gospel.'[3] The question here raised
is no longer that of the dependence of the Gospel on the unity of
the Church, but that of its dependence on the Church *simpliciter*.
Zwingli refutes Augustine, or at least the view ascribed by supporters of the Church's authority to Augustine, by asking how
St. Matthew's Gospel, which, according to a tradition which
Zwingli accepts, was written in the ninth year after the Ascension
to supply the needs of the Church, could possibly have been dependent for its authority on the Church. He concludes, after
further discussion: 'For how could it be that divine things should
take their authority from human things? And how would it not
be the deepest impiety to think that what sprang from the mouth
of God, not man, was not established unless human ignorance
had agreed?'[4] Of course, by substituting 'divine things' for 'Scripture' and 'human things' for 'Church', he has begged the question, and no one could give any other answer to the questions
which he poses than the one which he implies, because of the way
in which he frames them; but Zwingli certainly regards himself as
having proved that the Scripture needs no approval from and is
independent of the Church.[5] Similarly, the first of the 67 Articles
prepared by Zwingli for the Disputation in 1523 states: 'All those
who say that the Gospel is nothing without the Churches' guarantee, err and insult God.'[6] This statement Zwingli undertakes

----

[1] *ap.* Zwingli, I, 267.

[2] This is shown by Zwingli's alternate use of *euangelion* and *scriptura*, e.g. in his answer
to the Bishop's forty-third section, I, 302; cf. I, 374, where he says that the 'Gospel'
includes everything revealed by God to men.

[3] Zwingli misquotes; Augustine wrote: '*ego vero euangelio non crederem, nisi me catholicae
ecclesiae commoveret auctoritas*'.

[4] This whole argument is in I, 292–4.

[5] We here merely state Zwingli's position. It is discussed *infra*, pp. 90, 91.

[6] I, 458.

to prove beyond doubt in the Expositions of the 67 Articles,
relying for his arguments as usual on the Scripture itself.

Wholly in accord with this is his method of treating the assertion of Martin Blantsch of Tübingen, made at the Disputation
itself: 'The Church, assembled in the Councils in the Holy Spirit,
cannot err.'[1] Zwingli replied in the first place by showing that
Councils had often erred, and urged that they need only be obeyed
when their decisions are in harmony with the Gospel. Then he
attacked the view that the Church cannot err. 'What Church is
meant when it is stated that the Church cannot err?' he asked.
'If it is the Church centred in the Pope and administered by the
Cardinals and the Bishops, I say that it has often erred, and often
errs'. Then he went on to say that there is another Church: 'This
Church is nothing but the total of all Christian believers,
assembled in the Spirit and the will of God, placing firm faith and
undoubting hope in God, its Bridegroom; this Church depends on
and abides in the Word and Will of God alone'. This Church,
said Zwingli, is certainly inerrant, because it does nothing in
accordance with its own desires, but always what the Holy Spirit
ordains; this is the true Church.[2] Thus Zwingli's contention was
that the Word is superior to the Church, even the true Church,
and that so far is the Word from being dependent on the Church
that the Church is preserved from error only in so far as it con-
forms to the Word and Will of God. Zwingli adheres to this line
of argument in the part of the *de vera et falsa Religione* (1525) devoted to the nature of the Church. Here also he speaks of two
Churches. The first is the whole company of nominal Christians—
the wheat and the tares growing together until the harvest, by no
means 'without spot and blemish'. The other is the true Church,
known only to God, described by Paul in the Epistle to the
Ephesians, the Bride of Christ, for whom Christ gave his life; this
Church is spread over the whole world, and relies on the word of
Christ alone. 'Here is the Church which cannot err.' And it is
incapable of error, says Zwingli, as being the Church 'which relies
on God alone'.[3]

It follows from this, of course, that the Word of God possesses
greater authority than Councils, Fathers, and Popes. That
Zwingli had no hesitation in drawing this conclusion appears from
the following and many other passages: 'In them [*sc.* the ancients,
i.e. the Fathers] you will find much that is alien and contrary to

[1] I, 534 (the Proceedings of the Disputation are in I, 479–569).
[2] I, 537, 538.   [3] III, 743–9.

the evangelical and apostolic writings. Should we believe the former or the latter? He will answer, unless he is a stock or stone, or brute beast: We should believe that which was handed down at the dictation of the Spirit of God.'[1] In answer to the Bishop of Constance's insistence that General Councils should be obeyed, Zwingli replies: 'By "General Councils" I do not know whether you wish to be understood the four which some people assert in tradition ought to be regarded as highly as the Gospel, or all of them, although I do not know how pious it is to wish the same faith ascribed to them as to the Gospel. . . . If all of them, I will ask you, whether you think that faith in all of them should be preserved and that they should be kept inviolate? If you say, "Yes", I beg you to resolve this problem, whether we ought to obey those which decreed . . . that a bishop should be the husband of one wife, or those which at the instigation of demons forbid marriage. Will it not be our duty on this point to have recourse to Scripture?'[2] Elsewhere he says: 'Yes, I recognize that Pope and Councils have often erred, especially Anastasius and Liberius in the error of Arius.'[3] Quite consistently with this, he admits that under certain well-defined conditions a Council makes no errors. He is answering the argument of his opponents that a Council which has asked God for a right understanding of the Scripture should be obeyed by all Christians, and says that majorities do not guarantee truth; but he goes on to concede: 'as often as a Council is assembled in the Spirit of God, it cannot err.' For, he adds, it will recognize in that case only what the Scripture indicates to be the truth.[4] Thus the Scripture is supreme, even when an infallible Council is sitting; for its infallibility is merely derivative.

The most obvious, and, indeed, almost the most powerful, objection to the Zwinglian, as well as to the Lutheran, doctrine of the Bible is that many passages in it are susceptible of more than one interpretation. Who, then, is to carry out the interpretation? And if it has to be done, surely the Church, with its abundant resources of experience and divine guidance, is best fitted to do it? The suggestion that anyone should become the interpreter of the Bible was for Zwingli intolerable, since it virtually subordinated the Bible to a human being, or body of human beings, and he takes up a great part of the *von der Klarheit und Gewissheit usw.* in rebutting it. He begins his discussion of the point by

---

[1] I, 260. Notice the 'theory of inspiration' in the last words.   [2] I, 302.
[3] I, 375 (1522).   [4] II, 25 (1523).

asserting: 'The Word of God, as soon as it shines upon the understanding of man, illuminates it in such a way that it understands
it, confesses it, and becomes certain of it.'[1] He establishes this
statement by numerous examples from the Scripture in which the
patriarchs and others had no difficulty in understanding the
commands of God, even when they contradicted the intimations
of human reason (we have seen, on p. 71, that Zwingli's argument
is here confused by his interpreting the 'Word of God' to include
the direct message of God to man, when he should have limited
it to the Scripture, but this does not alter the point which he is
making).[2] He comes later to deal with his opponents' suggestion
from another angle. They admit, he says, that they, as Christians,
must accept the teaching of the Gospel, but urge that they understand the Gospel differently, and that therefore there must be
someone to decide between him and them and reduce the erring
party to silence. 'A true, natural meaning belongs to God's
words. . . . A man must subject his own nature to the Word of
God, and it will bring to birth in you and me its own meaning.
And it is possible to confute those in error by the simple method
of bringing them to the fountain-head, although they are not very
willing to come to it. Moreover, some people are so firmly sewn
into their asses' skin that when the natural meaning is made plain
to them, so that they cannot contradict it, they say that they cannot take the passage in this way, unless the Fathers have come to
the conclusion that it must be so understood; for it must be the
case that many people understand a thing better than one or a
few. The answer to them is: if that were the case, Christ must have
been false, for the majority of the priesthood was of a different
opinion from his. . . .'[3] Thus Zwingli maintains that there is no
difficulty at all about the interpretation of the Scripture, though
he does admit that the reader must approach the text in the
proper frame of mind: 'place all your hope of comfort in the Lord
Jesus Christ, that is, be certain that, since he has suffered for us,
he is the atonement for us in the sight of God in eternity';[4] 'a
man must subject his own nature to the Word of God'.[5] If these
conditions are fulfilled, the Word of God will convey its true
meaning directly to the heart and mind of the reader. Therefore no
interpreter is necessary: 'completely worthless are the unconsidered
statements of those who maintain that there must be a judge to
decide which is the proper understanding of the Scripture, as if

<hr>

[1] I, 361.   [2] I, 362 sqq.   [3] I, 374, 375.
[4] I, 374.   [5] I, 374 (just quoted).

one should or could give judgement on the Word of God',[1] as he
says elsewhere.

Zwingli wrote these last words after the Disputation of
29th January 1523, as part of his Expositions of the 67 Articles
which he had prepared and published in the previous year for
discussion at the Disputation. Now, of course, both before and
during the Disputation itself he vehemently maintained, in accordance with his belief in the supreme authority and absolute
clarity of the Word of God, that the Scripture and the Scripture
alone could and must decide all questions under dispute. Similarly, having been invited to a Disputation at Baden on 16th May
1526, he replied by laying down seven conditions for the proper
conduct of a theological disputation, and among them this: 'no
judges shall be set up over God's Word, nor over those who speak
on the spot out of God's Word.'[2] But in the course of the 1523
Disputation he had been forced by the difficulty of the position
which he had taken up to make two modifications in it, one
temporary and one permanent. The temporary one was, perhaps, of small importance. Against the Vicar of Constance's
claim that Fathers and Councils should be listened to, he urged,
of course, that only the Scripture could decide a point; but he
added later in the course of his argument: 'We have in this city of
Zürich—God be praised!—as many learned friends, sufficiently
practised in the three before-mentioned languages [sc. Hebrew,
Greek, and Latin], as in any of the Universities mentioned by the
Vicar. . . . Also there sit here in this room doctors of the Divine
Scripture, doctors in spiritual law, many learned men from many
Universities. These shall hear and have read out the Scripture
which is quoted, in order to establish whether that which is tested
and pronounced on the authority of the Scripture is really true.
And if all this were nothing, there are in this assembly so many
Christian hearts, instructed by the Holy Ghost, and of such good
understanding, that they can easily in accordance with the Spirit
of God judge and recognize which party rightly or wrongly
quotes the Scripture to support its view, or tries to force it violently
against its proper meaning.'[3] But we need not take this apparent
subordination of the Word of God to doctors and ordinary
Christians too seriously. If Zwingli had been attacked on this
point, he would doubtless have replied that the function of the
assessors was not, strictly, that of interpreting and judging the
Scripture, but that of hearing the Scripture in the right frame of

[1] II, 26, 27 (July 1523).   [2] V, 13.   [3] I, 498, 499.

mind and allowing it to bring to birth its meaning in their minds, and then of deciding whether the disputants had really done the same thing, or had approached the Scripture with preconceived ideas and forced it to mean what they wanted it to mean. No doubt even this is a dangerous concession to those who insist on the need of an interpretation of the Scripture, but, as Zwingli does not elsewhere make it, we may reasonably suppose that it never became part of the texture of his thought, and was perhaps dictated as much by courtesy to his audience as by anything else.

The permanent and more important modification of his view that the Scripture's meaning is always so plain that it needs no interpreter occurred after a long argument as to whether the Mass was a sacrifice or not; each side supported its view by Scriptural quotation, and Zwingli's opponents were quick to make their usual suggestion that a judge would have to decide the issue. Zwingli, as usual, repudiated the idea with vigour, and the Vicar replied that the doctrines of Arius and Sabellius would still be flourishing if recourse had not been had to judges who declared their views incompatible with Scripture. Zwingli retorted that the Fathers, in order to deal with these heretics, had used the same method precisely which he insisted on—proof from the Scripture and the Scripture alone. For Arius—and here we reach the operative passage—quoted Scripture to prove his case: 'The Father is greater than I' (John xiv. 28). Thereupon the Fathers adduced such passages as 'I and the Father are one'(John x. 30), and triumphantly established that the passage quoted by Arius referred to the humanity, not the divinity of Christ. In other words they worked by the principle: 'the Scripture expounds the Scripture'.[1] Thus Zwingli has advanced from saying that the Scripture's meaning is absolutely plain to saying that when one passage is obscure its meaning is to be elucidated by another passage in the Scripture. This idea receives explicit formulation among the seven conditions laid down by Zwingli in 1526 for a proper disputation: The Word of God shall not be treated violently by mere intellect and exposition, but, if it is obscure in any place, it is to be expounded by God's Word from another place.[2]

Nagel contends that this conception, which, if fully developed, implies that the Bible is an organic whole, first emerged with

---

[1] I, 555–61, especially 560, 561; the original of the last few words is: *'legt geschrifft die geschrifft uss.'*

[2] V, 12.

complete clarity in Zwingli's mind as a result of the controversy with Luther and his views.[1] This can scarcely be the case, as we have just found it clearly expressed two or three years before the controversy with Luther broke out in 1525–6. But it is true that it played a prominent part in Zwingli's writings against Luther before the Marburg Conference of 1529.[2] And at the Conference it furnished Zwingli's main line of argument. While Luther constantly harped on the words, 'This is My body', and said that their meaning was so plain that nothing would move him from his interpretation of them, Zwingli sought to establish his own interpretation of them by quoting other passages from the Scripture. This meant, of course, a protracted deadlock. Zwingli eventually made another attempt to end it by charging Luther with begging the question by assuming that his interpretation of 'This is My body' was correct and refusing to argue the point. 'An argumentative man, on your principles, could say that John was the son of Mary—for Christ said "Behold your son"—by persistently repeating, "Christ said, Behold your son, behold your son." ' 'I am not begging the question', said Luther; 'for one article of faith is not proved by another.' 'The Scriptures are to be compared, and their meanings to be discovered from the Scriptures themselves', replied Zwingli.[3]

This principle, that obscure passages in the Bible can and must be cleared up by reference to other passages, saved Zwingli, in his own eyes, from the charge of sheer individualism—that he was exalting his own interpretation of the Bible above the Church and the Bible itself—as well as finally disposing of the need to accept the Fathers or Councils or the Church as arbiters on disputed points in Holy Writ; and it enabled him to maintain against all comers the Scripture's independence of the Church and superiority to it.

But it is not his last word on the interpretation of Scripture. The Eucharistic controversy caused him to think out all his presuppositions very clearly, and in particular it forced him to consider whether he had any secure ground from which to contest Luther's interpretation of the Eucharistic passages of Scripture. The *words* of Matthew xxvi. 26, 'This is My body', taken in and by themselves, could as well be taken in Luther's sense as in his,

---

[1] *Zwinglis Stellung zur Schrift*, Ch. IV.

[2] *vide* e.g. V, 603 sq. (from the *Amica Exegesis*, 1527).

[3] Rodolphus Collinus' account of the Marburg Conference is given by Kidd, *Documents of the Continental Reformation*, No. 109, pp. 247–54.

and perhaps they could be better taken thus. How demonstrate that his interpretation was the correct one? We have seen that Zwingli's chief resource was to insist on the method of comparing Scripture with Scripture, and perhaps this was enough. But Zwingli tried also another approach. In the *Amica Exegesis* of 1527 he methodically confuted Luther's views on the Sacrament where they conflicted with his own, and set out his own. In his *Sermon von dem Sacrament*, Luther had said: 'He who forms the true faith from the words, believes thus: Whether Christ creeps down into the bread or the cup or wherever he will, if I have the words, I do not wish to see or think further.'[1] Zwingli replied that faith cannot be formed from the words of the Bible, but that the latter are to be understood under the guidance of faith and must yield to faith. He further stated that Luther had himself put forward this principle, but was now no longer loyal to it.[2] Thus the principle has emerged that faith is the true interpreter of Scripture. (This is true in so far as a man of Christian faith is probably in general better fitted to understand the Bible, than a man without this faith, by whom the Bible was never taken seriously; but since each man's interpretation is likely to differ from every other man's, we should end by leaving the matter always to the individual's judgement and scarcely be able to expound the Scriptures at all except to ourselves.)

The Word of God, in Zwingli's view, was not only superior in authority to the Church, it also dominated the life of the Church, and we must now turn to his view of the relation between the Word of God and the Church as properly constituted. We have already seen (on p. 75) that he distinguished between two 'Churches'. But if we are to appreciate his full view, we must notice that he believed the word 'Church' to be used in three senses, and it is by elucidating these three senses that we shall best understand his conception of the true Church. The first sense is that of the company of all professing Christians, i.e. the Church governed by the Pope and the hierarchy descending from him. This is in Zwingli's opinion no true Church at all, and having noticed that in Zwingli's writings and thought the word Church sometimes refers to this we need here spend no further time on it. The Church in the second sense has already been described in outline (on p. 75); it should here be added that

[1] *W.A.*, XIX, 485.

[2] V, 663; cf., in the same work, V, 625, where Zwingli says that we are to use the 'rule of faith and a simple knowledge of the faith' for understanding the Bible. *Vide* on this matter W. Köhler, *Zwingli and Luther*, I, 475.

F

this Church, although it is 'without spot or blemish' and contains within itself only the genuine followers of Christ, is yet not ideal, but real, not invisible, but visible, for it exists and has existed wherever the Christian life has been lived and is being lived;[1] it is known, however, only to God, and will never come visibly together until the final day of human history.[2] This is the 'catholic' or 'universal' Church, the 'Communion of all faithful people'.[3]

The third use of the word 'Church' is to describe the individual communities or congregations into which the universal Church is divided. Since the power of the keys was given by Christ to all the Apostles, it was given in them to all believers. The keys are the preaching of the pure Gospel and the liberation and comforting of the soul, which thus belongs to all believers. This is Zwingli's conception of the 'Priesthood of all believers'. This means that a community, or *Gemeinde*, formed of believers, is, in virtue of the priestly office attaching to each member, autonomous, and each *Gemeinde* has exactly the same amount of authority and power as each other *Gemeinde*. It organizes itself, therefore, and controls the lives of its members without interference from any outside agency or person, although it uses only spiritual weapons to enforce its will. Although all Christians are priests, they are not all apostles or prophets; therefore no man may take the office of preacher and pastor on himself. If a man is called to preach by Christ, he is appointed as preacher by the *Gemeinde*, which is entrusted by God with the right to recognize and legitimize his call. In effect, thus, the *Gemeinde* has full powers to choose and dismiss its preachers, though it is those, and only those, who have received God's special gift for the purpose who are to be chosen by it. While the preachers are in office, the message which they preach is to be tested by the *Gemeinde*, and any other preacher whose message does not conform to the proper standard is, of course, dismissed by the *Gemeinde*.[4]

Both the universal Church and the individual *Gemeinde* are controlled and regulated by the Word of God. The universal Church derives all its authority, as we have seen (on p. 75), from its unswerving obedience to the will of God revealed in His Word, and, in fact, ceases to be the true Church and becomes instead the 'nominal' Church as soon as it departs in any particular from that

---

[1] *Ubi Christo vivitur*, III, 750. (*de vera et falsa Religione*, 1525.)

[2] ibid.   [3] III, 751; cf. II, 571.

[4] For a full account of Zwingli's doctrine of the Church, *vide* A. Farner, *Die Lehre von Kirche und Staat bei Zwingli*, Erster Teil.

obedience. The description just given of the *Gemeinde* perhaps gives the impression of a democratic community whose institutions and laws are the expression of the general will and which is answerable for its decisions and its actions to no one and nothing. But such an impression would be far removed from the truth. Like the universal Church of which it forms a part, it is bound hand and foot to the Word of God. Its institutions and the manner of life which it demands of its members are prescribed by the Word, as we see from the fact that Zwingli grounds every reform which he suggests for the city of Zürich explicitly on the teaching of the Scripture, and argues each detail with his opponents from that point of view and that point of view alone. There is no question of 'self-determination' or democracy in the manner in which it arrives at its decision. No doubt in practice a vote had often to be taken and the majority's wish regarded as the wish of the community, but in theory the Word of God, which 'is seated in the minds of the faithful',[1] decides the issue unaided. This is in particular true of the appointment, testing, and dismissal of preachers and pastors; for the preacher is the Word of God's organ of expression; if the message which the candidate or preacher preaches tallies with the inner Word which the *Gemeinde* possesses,[2] then he is the true organ of the Word and can be appointed to or retained in his office; if not, he is not the true organ of the Word, and the *Gemeinde*, which is entrusted with the recognition of the fact, cannot allow him to hold the office of preacher.[3] There is perhaps one point in which the decisions of the community are not dominated by the Word: it is not easy to see how the divine call of the preacher, as opposed to the message which he preaches, can be tested by the Word of God, and Zwingli does not say that it is; here surely the *Gemeinde* must use the direct gift of the Spirit. But in all other respects the Word regulates the life and thought of the Christian community.

This was Zwingli's original and characteristic theory of the Church, and he genuinely attempted to put it without modification into practice. Until 1525 his reforms were carried out in and through the *Gemeinden*, with only such assistance from the State as his theory of the State allowed. But the pressure of events gradually compelled him to modify his practice, and, in accordance

---

[1] III, 752.

[2] The inner Word, 'seated' or 'written' in the minds of the faithful, is, of course, identical with the Bible; there is no theory of 'inner light' here.

[3] I, 756.

therewith, his theory also. These modifications were of such a kind that they involved modifications of his theory and practice with regard to the State also, and so we shall best understand them if we first propound Zwingli's original and characteristic view of the State and the Word of God's relation to it.

Zwingli, like the other great Reformers, was strongly opposed to anarchy in every guise. He is at great pains to prove from Scripture that the magistracy is ordained by God (not the Word of God, be it noted). The Scriptural passages taken by some to rule out the necessity of having or obeying magistrates are really designed, he points out, to condemn tyranny, not magistracy as such; and there are many passages which emphasize the obligation of Christians to obey the properly constituted authority. He is equally insistent that the view is false which asserts that no Christian can hold a magistracy; on the contrary, only a Christian can be a good magistrate.[1] As regards the structure of a State, Zwingli affirms that in external matters it closely resembles the true Church; for in it each must care for the welfare of the whole; dangers, and sometimes good fortune, must be shared; no one may use his gifts exclusively for his own benefit, and no one may stir up strife.[2] A State will be happy only if true religion be found in it.[3] The duties of a magistrate are discussed, and those of the subject in relation to him; even an impious magistrate is a minister of God for the execution of justice and must be obeyed, unless he give an order in contradiction to the will of God; in which case he may be deposed.[4] The magistrate is, of course, entitled to use force in the carrying out of his functions, acting as the servant of God in the punishment of crime.[5] The Church and all matters of religion are independent of the State. But if the State is Christian it has the duty in an emergency, but only in an emergency, to come to the assistance of the Church. When it does this, it must act without force, for there must be no compulsion in the sphere of religion.[6]

We may notice about this theory of the State that Zwingli does not explicitly place the magistrates under the direct domination of the Word. They are entitled, it appears, to carry out the

[1] III, 867–77 (from the *de vera et falsa Religione*, 1525, as are the next four references).
[2] III, 867, 868. [3] III, 868.
[4] III, 880–8; cf. Articles 37, 38, and 42 of the Sixty-seven Articles (I, 462, 463).
[5] III, 883, 884; cf. Article 40 (I, 462).
[6] This is stated on the authority of A. Farner, op. cit., Dritter Teil, and his references are at the moment impossible to obtain; but the idea that the State should at times interfere follows naturally from Article 14 (I, 459): 'all Christians are to take the greatest pains to ensure that the Gospel of Christ alone is preached everywhere.'

ordinary business of government according to the principles which
seem best to them, so long as they do not enjoin anything which a
Christian must regard as contrary to the will of God. The State
has its independent authorization directly from God, and this
authorization carries it through the execution of its ordinary
tasks. There is no reason to think that a preacher with a Bible in
his hand can dictate to the magistrates from the law of Moses
what they ought to do, shall we say, in the matter of public health.

As in the case of his doctrine of the Church, so here also Zwingli
genuinely sought to put his theory into practice in the early stages
of his reforming activity. Realizing that all efforts to prevail upon
the official Church to call a General Council were destined to be
fruitless, and convinced therefore that an emergency in the affairs
of the Church had arisen, he called upon the Council of Zürich
for its assistance and asked it to summon an assembly for the free
discussion of debated religious matters. Having called this
assembly, the Council had finished, in his view, its function in the
matter. It is true that the Council, after the Disputation in question, that of 29th January 1523, published a decree requiring all
preachers to conform to the standard of Holy Scripture,[1] but it
did this, on Zwingli's showing, in fulfilment of its function to
preserve order in the State and prevent faction. Similarly, the
Council called the assembly for the Second Disputation, later in
the same year, in virtue of its right and duty to assist the Church
in a time of emergency, and, similarly, the Council put out, in
the course of the Disputation, a Mandate for the abolition of
images and the Mass.[2] In other words, in both cases, the
Gemeinden of Zürich were reforming themselves; when they indicated what reforms they desired, it became necessary for the
State, in the interests of law and order, the preservation of which
was its God-given province, to give its authority for the carrying
out of these reforms. Until 1525 all reforms were carried out in
this co-operative manner, both Church and State remaining
true to their proper functions.

But the *Gemeinden*, endowed with full independence by
Zwingli, did not in every case desire precisely what Zwingli
expected them to desire, or, as he would have put it, did not wish
to conform at all points to the Word of God. In particular, the
Mass was still celebrated in various parts of the city according to
the old formularies. Zwingli called on the Council to abolish the
Mass by active, though non-violent, intervention. By a small

[1] I, 469.   [2] II, 678.

majority the necessary decree was passed, and on 12th April
1525, the last Mass was said in Zürich. This appeal to the
Council was in clear contravention of Zwingli's own principles,
for the civil authority was asked to set on one side the wishes of
individual *Gemeinden*. Zwingli defended himself on the ground
that an emergency had again arisen, but this defence is clearly
inadequate. No doubt his opponents had claimed other actions on
Zwingli's and the Council's parts to be infringements of Zwinglian
principles, but here was a clear case.

The State, having entered into the spiritual realm, continued at
Zwingli's request to make its presence there more and more felt.
The troubles with the Anabaptists in 1525 and the following years
caused Zwingli to make repeated appeals for intervention to the
civil authority. The order for the drowning of obdurate Anabaptists, on 7th March 1526, though no doubt it could be defended on the ground that their activity was causing civil dis-
order, was dangerously like compulsion in matters of faith, against
which Zwingli had declared himself in the past. But just as significant as the irruption of the State into religious affairs was that
of the Church, in the person principally of Zwingli himself, into
secular affairs. The path towards theocracy had been struck out,
and it was thereafter steadily followed; by 1528 the end of the
journey had been reached, though Zwingli was still apparently
unconscious, if we may judge from his writings of that year, that
his conception of the *Gemeinde* had been altered. The constitution
of 1528 shows the city ruled in religious and secular affairs alike
by one authority in the form of a Council; and the Council is
headed by the prophet, Zwingli. His writings from this time forth
show the greater and greater influence exerted on him by the
figures of the Old Testament prophets, and in his latest writings
the prophet appears as above the Church and the worldly
authority alike.

But the prophet is, of course, the organ of the Word of God; all
his words and activities in that capacity are derived from that
Word. Therefore the rule of Zwingli in the city of Zürich was the
rule of the Word, dominant in worldly and spiritual affairs alike;
the Bible is found to contain the law of the State as it had been
previously found to contain the law of the Church.

So far as the change in Zwingli's theories is concerned, he has
altered his idea of the relation of the Word to the Church only in
so far as he has now given the Word a personal embodiment; but
the relation of the Word to the State is fundamentally altered by

the suggestion that the Word now does not merely confirm the
view that the State is ordained of God, but actually directs it in
the carrying out of all its tasks. We have described Zwingli's
original view on both these points as being also characteristic,
since it was largely unaffected by the harsh realities of political
and religious conflict; but if we would have a full idea of Zwingli's
thought we may not leave his later view out of account, and some
would say that the beliefs fashioned out of the necessities of life
are more genuine than the products of the study.

Before we can believe ourselves to have done full justice to
Zwingli's doctrine of authority, we must refer to a current of his
thought which has so far gone unmentioned, as being alien to its
main stream. Sabatier rightly draws attention to this passage in
the *de vera et falsa Religione:* 'Thou seest where the cold cavils of
the Papists and the priests will end when they affirm that the
meaning of the celestial Word depends on the judgement of men.
Thou canst never know what is the Church which can never err
nor decay, if thou recognizest not the Word of God who constituted the Church. This Word has the virtue of giving faith in
the Church, it can remove her errors, it permits the acceptance of
no other Word. Only pious hearts know this, for faith does not
depend on the discussion of men, but has its seat and rests itself
invincibly in the soul. It is an experience which everyone may
have. It is not a doctrine, or question of knowledge, for we see the
most learned men who are ignorant of this thing which is the most
salutary of all.'[1] He concludes from it that this is ultimately the
theology of experience, not of authority (i.e. external authority).[2]
It is clear that here Zwingli seems to go back behind the authority
of the Word of God to that of the personal experience of the
believer, who knows directly what neither the arguments of
learned men nor the Scripture itself have taught him. If it seems
that Sabatier is extracting too much from the passage, his view
may be supported by the quotation of several other passages from
Zwingli's earlier writings. We have seen before (on pp. 70 and
71) that in the *von der Klarheit und Gewissheit usw.* he is sometimes confused between two possible meanings of the 'Word of
God', as meaning the Scripture and as meaning the message of
God spoken directly to the individual soul. The very fact that he
admitted the latter as a possible meaning of the phrase is almost

---

[1] III, 749 (the translation is that of Sabatier's translator).

[2] A. Sabatier, *Religions of Authority and the Religion of the Spirit* (English translation),
I, 163.

sufficient to show that he believed it possible to know the truth without the mediation of the written or even the preached Word. And various sentences and paragraphs in the course of the passage in question put this beyond doubt. 'Listen: the Apostles cherish no doubt, but, taught by God, not by men, say: we believe and know. Yes, if you would wish to say: "if only God had taught me!" I answer: I perceive that God has not taught you, for if he had taught you, you would know for certain, as did the disciples, that you had been taught by God. . . . If you ask further: how ought I to reach the point of being taught by him, so that I know for certain that this or that opinion accords with his will, my answer is the same; Desire it from him, and he will give it to you, and it will profit you.'[1] Similarly, when he imagines someone as raising the question as to how he can be sure that he has attained the right interpretation of a Scriptural passage, he answers it by saying: 'Seek God in your inner chamber (Matthew vi. 6), and there secretly pray to him; he sees you well, so that he can give you understanding of his truth. For . . . we can learn from no one more certainly what the meaning of the Word of God is than from God himself.'[2] And there is more than a trace of reliance on personal experience at the end of the treatise, where Zwingli gives twelve criteria by which the listener to a sermon can be sure that the preacher is truly preaching the Word of God, and the reader of the Bible that he himself is obtaining the true sense of the passage. For instance, the listener and the reader are to ask themselves whether they feel God to be becoming dearer to them, whether they feel surer of the peace of God and themselves to be of lesser importance in their own eyes.[3] This is surely to test the Word of God by personal feeling, and not personal feeling by the Word of God.[4]

These passages are all from the earlier writings of Zwingli, and the idea is not easily discoverable, if it is discoverable at all, in his writings after 1525. Nagel[5] is probably right in suggesting that the controversies with the Anabaptists, with their much vaunted 'prophesyings' and personal revelations, made it urgently necessary to Zwingli to objectivize the Word of God, and to make no concessions to the doctrine of individual illumination. In any case the idea is foreign to the main trend of his thought. Yet it

---

[1] I, 367.   [2] I, 375, 376.   [3] I, 383, 384.

[4] cf. Zwingli's account of his own 'enlightenment', given on p. 65, *supra*. There also God speaks directly to the soul.

[5] *Zwinglis Stellung zur Schrift*, Ch. III.

springs quite naturally from Zwingli's own personal religious experience, and might have played a much greater part in the system of his thought if the cast of his mind, and, perhaps, the conditions of his controversies, had been different.

We may now sum up Zwingli's answer to the problem of authority. The Word of God, in the historical and concrete form of the canonical Scriptures, is to him the sole and wholly authoritative source of religious truth; the validity of any religious statement not actually contained within the pages of the Bible is wholly derivative from and dependent upon the Bible. Within the Bible the Old and New Testaments are of equal validity and authority. The Bible, moreover, regulates the whole life of the Church, and at the same time the religious life of the individual, which is lived in the context of the Church. The State, in the early stages of Zwingli's mature thought, has its authorization direct from God and follows its own laws; in the later stages it also comes under the régime of the Bible, and the Bible becomes also the law of political and economic life.

If we try to pick out the differences between Luther's view and his, we notice firstly that Zwingli's moves in a much more intellectual atmosphere: it is an inference directly and logically drawn from an intellectual position arrived at after a long process of reflection; Luther reached his view by deriving it, as much by the aid of passion and under the stimulus of urgent practical necessity as by means of a strictly logical process, from a conviction which was at least as emotional as it was intellectual. Secondly, Zwingli does not distinguish, by means of a criterion derived from personal experience or of any other, between the Word of God and the canonical Scriptures. Thirdly, Zwingli does not, except in the latest stages of his thought, give to the Word of God the same totalitarian status that Luther does and assign to it the domination of all parts of life; in other words he goes much farther than Luther in the direction of breaking up the medieval unity in which the distinctions of Church and State, sacred and secular, were contained, and of preparing the way for the departmental conception of life which is characteristic of the modern world.

III

Will Zwingli's answer to the problem of authority hold? It is clear that it resembles Luther's so closely that a great deal of what has been said about the latter (on pp. 55–61) applies with equal force to it, and need not be repeated here. In the first place, then, we can at once assert that Zwingli's view shares with Luther's what we have seen to be the great merit of seeking to objectivize the content of religious faith. We may go on at once to consider the question whether his attempt is more successful than Luther's.

It is not open to the objection, as was Luther's, that it turns out to be nothing more than the elevation of one man's personal experience to the level of an authoritative source of religious truth. The Scripture, in Zwingli's view, was a quite definite and concrete body of writings, written long before Zwingli's time, and—which is more important when we compare Zwingli with Luther—defined as to its limits long before Zwingli's time. The traditional objection to this view is that the canon was fixed by the decision of the Church, that therefore the Church virtually decided what the Word of God is by rejecting the claims of many writings and admitting the claims of a few to be included within the Word of God; and that in consequence the authority of the Church must be above that of the Bible, and if the Bible has any authority at all it must be derivative from that of the Church. This objection is plausible only if we define with great care the meaning of the word 'Church' in this instance; the Councils of the Church did not 'fix' the Canon of Scripture—that is to say, they did not decide points which were disputed within the Church. Rather, they formulated and reasserted decisions which had been gradually reached by the great body of Christians on the ground of their personal and corporate experience of God since the foundation of the Church. This personal and corporate experience of God was therefore the deciding factor, and is in fact what the word 'Church' means in this instance. Thus the objection to Zwingli fully and plausibly stated is that to assert the authority of the Scripture is, logically, to assert the prior and superior authority of the personal and corporate experience of God given to the great body of Christians from the foundation of the Church until the fixing of the Canon of Holy Scripture; it is therefore impossible to maintain the absolute authority of the Scripture.

We know what was Zwingli's answer to this objection from the passage in the *Apologeticus Archeteles* (already cited on p. 74) in which Zwingli deals with his adversaries' contention that the Gospel depends on the unity of the Church. In the course of this he claims, at least by implication, that the authority of the Gospel cannot possibly depend on the Church in any shape or form because it was dictated to men by the Holy Spirit; all that the Church could do was to admit that this was so, and if it did not do so that would only be so much the worse for the Church. Thus the Word of God must be authoritative, since it is, in fact, the pronouncement of the Holy Spirit.[1] To this we must reply: it may or may not be the case that the Holy Spirit dictated His message to the Scriptural writers; if He did, the Zwinglian conclusion, of course, follows. But the very question to which we are seeking an answer is whether He did so or not, whether the truth was in some way revealed to these writers. Who is to tell us? The writers themselves, or the personal and corporate experience of the great body of Christians, or Luther's evangelical experience, or Zwingli, or the Council of Trent, or our own inner light, or something that we have not yet discovered? In other words, we are thrown back on the problem of authority in one of its acutest forms.

But Zwingli's answer to the objection can be re-stated in a less vulnerable form. The Bible is the Word of God, and therefore authoritative; this statement does not depend on the concrete fact that the Holy Spirit dictated the Bible to its writers, which cannot be finally established as a fact; it is the object of faith, like the existence of God and the redemption achieved by Jesus Christ. A man or a community either has this faith or does not have it; the Church in the early centuries had it, and therefore asserted that the Sacred Canon consisted of certain books and no others; Zwingli had it; those who dispute the Bible's authority do not have it. Therefore the authority of the Bible is not derived from that of the Church or from any source whatsoever.

There is no doubt that this form of Zwingli's answer does meet the objection, and is in itself unassailable by argument, unless we are prepared to say that it makes the individual's faith, which is at the mercy of every 'wind of teaching', the final authority. But even if we are not prepared to say this, we can at any rate surely demand that an object of faith should be consistent with what we scientifically know about the universe, with a rational view of the universe and with other objects of faith. It must be maintained that the belief that the Bible is supremely authoritative is not so consistent, and that the arguments adduced against Luther's solution to the problem of authority on pp. 58–60 show that it is not so consistent.

[1] I, 293, 294.

If so, we must regretfully conclude that Zwingli has not solved the problem for us, although the suggestion that the authority of the Bible is an object of faith is not without its importance; and must now turn hopefully to Calvin.

CHAPTER III

CALVIN

I

WHEN we ask about John Calvin the question, To what extent, if at all, and in what sense did he recognize the problem of authority? we move into the presence of the most influential of all the Reformers. Whether he was also the greatest is a query which we need not put to ourselves, since all answers to it depend so much on the meaning which we attach to the word 'greatness'. But in religion, theology, politics, sociology, and economics his influence goes far beyond anything which any other Reformer was within measurable distance of achieving. In religion he, and the Geneva which he created, determined the type of devotion which characterizes historical Protestantism, persecuted, tolerated or triumphant, sectarian or 'established', in all non-Lutheran countries on both sides of the Atlantic.[1] His theology, at least until the rise of liberalism, and now again in reaction from it, has dominated the pulpits and lecture-rooms of Protestantism, even while the doctrine of Predestination has been gradually abandoned. In politics, modern ideas of democracy and the rights of the individual derive much of their power from the habituation of Calvinist minds to self-government. And in sociology and economics, few can doubt the close connexion between the Calvinistic virtues of thrift and industry, on the one hand, and the growth of modern commercialism and industrialism and the civilization in which they thrive, on the other.[2] Of course, many other forces, mostly invisible and incalculable, were also at work in producing the modern situation in these spheres of human thought and activity; but the personal influence of Calvin has been very great. But it is in the matter of Church government, which belongs to no one of the parts of life already mentioned, but is compounded out of all of them, that his influence has been, and remains, most profound and far-reaching.

The personality of Calvin is not particularly attractive to the modern mind, perhaps because he fails to make that appeal to the imagination which an unimaginative age perpetually seeks. He entered into the conflict of the Reformation after the first assaults

---

[1] *vide* M. Piette, *John Wesley in the Evolution of Protestantism, passim.*
[2] *vide* R. H. Tawney, *Religion and the Rise of Capitalism, passim.*

had been made, and the first counter-attacks had been resisted. The creative ideas and the emotional impetus of Lutheranism had already invaded many spheres of life and in many places were in full possession. It was to Lutheran religion that Calvin was converted.[1] His task was that of perpetuating and extending by organization and consolidation what had been gained. For this task he was eminently fitted by nature and training. He had little power of imagination or creative thought; he had immense powers of systematization. These powers were not limited, as they usually are, to the realm of practical affairs; they embraced equally the realm of philosophic thought. The excellence of the *Institutes of the Christian Religion* lies in its achievement of systematization and synthesization, not in its contribution of new ideas in any subject. Calvin accepted the half-formulated theology of Lutheranism, and worked out and set forth with supreme lucidity its fullest implications. In practical matters he had the advantage, which no other Reformer so completely had, of living in a city in which he could work out to the full, without any interruption or opposition that was not eventually eliminated, his own plans; but the credit belongs to him of discovering and putting into practice a system which applied not only to the limited situation of Geneva, but to many different situations in many different parts of the world.

We must be careful not to ascribe Protestant leanings to Calvin too early in his life. During his five years of theological study at the University of Paris, from 1523 to 1528, he betrayed, and almost certainly felt, no opposition to the faith of his fathers, although his sojourn in the somewhat repressive and reactionary atmosphere of the Collège de Montaigu (1524–8), at an age of his life when the human spirit begins to reach towards freedom in matters of thought, may have produced some kind of unconscious rebellion. Beza, in his first *Life of Calvin*,[2] asserts that Calvin was not sorry to abandon theology for the law at his father's request in 1528, partly because he had been unsettled in his faith by the influence of his cousin, older than himself, Pierre Robert, usually known as Olivetan, who was studying in Paris at the time.[3] It is true that Olivetan publicly embraced Reformed ideas very shortly afterwards, and was a man capable of exerting a profound

---

[1] So Troeltsch, *Die Sociallehre der Christlichen Kirchen* (English translation), II, 579.

[2] 19th August 1564.

[3] *Calvini Opera* (Brunswick edition; in the *Corpus Reformatorum*), XXI, 29. All further references to Calvin's works are to this edition.

influence on his friends. But nowhere, even in the prefaces which he contributed to Olivetan's translation of the Bible, does Calvin state that any religious influence of the kind required was exerted on him by his cousin.

Calvin did not stay long at Orleans, whither he repaired to study law, but was soon attracted by the fame of Alciat to Bourges. He was not impressed by the actual performance of his new professor, and would have left Bourges within a very short time had he not met there an Orleans friend, Melchior Wolmar, who had now settled at Bourges. Wolmar taught him Greek and perhaps Hebrew, and, being already a Lutheran, probably introduced him to the study of the New Testament in its original language. Roemond de Florimond, a very hostile historian of the Reformation, says that on the battlements of Bourges Wolmar advised Calvin to forsake the Code of Justinian for the Gospel of Jesus Christ, with results disastrous to Christianity.[1] Beza's second life of Calvin[2] may be held to support this statement by saying that Calvin formed a friendship with Wolmar 'in the name of religion'.[3] But de Florimond's statement is very probably founded on *a priori* notions of what Wolmar, being a Lutheran, is likely to have taught Calvin. At any rate, there is nothing in Calvin's proceedings to denote any change of heart or mind as yet; and when in 1546 Calvin dedicated his *Commentary on 2 Corinthians* to Wolmar and recorded with gratitude his debt to him, he mentioned many intellectual and personal services rendered to him by Wolmar, but said nothing of any religious influence.[4]

March 1531 found him back in Paris, but only for a short time, as his father's fatal illness called him to Noyon within the next six weeks. Gérard Cauvain (which seems to be the way in which Calvin senior spelt his name) had for several years been engaged in a weary wrangle with the local Chapter, and it was this wrangle that had caused him to bid John give up theology in 1528. The matter was still unsettled at his death, and he died excommunicate, though the quarrel was patched up sufficiently after his decease to allow him to be buried in consecrated ground. The rights and wrongs of the affair are irrecoverable after the lapse of centuries, though it appears that the Chapter had a *prima facie* case for condemning Gérard; but if we may suppose that John took his father's part in the matter, it may well be that

---

[1] *L'Histoire de la naissance, progréz et décadence de l'hérésie de ce siécle* (1605), p. 882.
[2] 1575.   [3] *'amicitiam religionis nomine iniit'* (XXI, 122).   [4] XII, 364.

the cloud which hung over his father's deathbed heightened the effect of the discussions which he had doubtless had with his humanistic and Reformed friends and tutors. But we cannot confidently say any more than this about the influence of his father's history. Yet perhaps it is not wholly illegitimate to suggest that the discontents which, according to his letter to Sadoleto in 1539, were making themselves felt for some time before his final conversion[1] were already beginning or had already begun. But in the same letter Calvin says that for a long time, offended by the novelty of the Reformed teaching, and restrained above all by his reverence for the Church, he at first strenuously resisted and afterwards for some time heard with reluctance the new-fangled teaching which was gaining currency.[2] Thus he was at this time, in all probability, in no sense a Reformed thinker, even if we are right in suggesting that he was disquieted by many of the things which he saw within the Church.

After the affairs of his father had been satisfactorily cleared up, Calvin returned to Paris, and, freed by his father's death from the obligation to study the law, for which he had no particular liking, although in some ways he may be said to have possessed a legal type of mind, he turned his attention to purely humanistic studies, and early in 1532 published at his own expense a commentary on Seneca's *de Clementia*. The surprising story is repeated by many of Calvin's early biographers that the work was written in order to recommend the French Lutherans to the mercy of their king, but this seems to be an inference based on the title of Seneca's work and a false analogy with the Preface to the *Institutes*. Doumergue is fantastically misguided when he asserts that the book shows clear proof that Calvin's conversion to Protestantism had already taken place.[3] The work is simply one of Classical scholarship, and quotes the Bible, each time from the Vulgate, only three times throughout, though it shows some knowledge of the Fathers. The absence from it of religious references does not prove, of course, that he was not yet converted; for why should he obtrude his religious convictions, however fresh they were to him, into such a work? But in default of direct evidence we shall be wise to conclude that his religious opinions had not yet made any decisive advance.

[1] V, 412. The passage, however, is not directly autobiographical (*vide* p. 98, *infra*) and should be used with caution.

[2] V, 412.

[3] E. Doumergue, *Jean Calvin*, I, 221. Beza, *Vita Calvini* (*Calvini Opera*, XXI, 123), puts the conversion before this date.

His conversion probably took place before the autumn of the following year, for we have a letter dated 27th October 1533, to Daniel, in which he asks his friend to exercise care in respect of certain papers connected with Reform activities in Paris, and refers to Gérard Roussel, their leader, as 'our Gérard'.[1] Calvin was definitely implicated in the effort on the following All Saints' Day of Nicholas Cop, the new Rector of the University of Paris, to set on foot a great Protestant movement by means of his inaugural discourse; for when the police were foiled in their attempt to arrest Cop on a charge of heresy, they looked for Calvin instead, and were thwarted only by his precipitate flight. This fact is properly explained only by the supposition that Calvin had been converted to Protestantism at least some weeks previously, probably some months. The attempt of Doumergue,[2] however, to assure us that he must have been converted at least as early as the preceding June, breaks down; it relies on the fact that Calvin on the 27th of that month held a serious conversation with a younger sister of Daniel who was about to enter a nunnery, and urged her not to do so unless she was quite sure of her vocation to it; surely any conscientious Catholic might have said what Calvin said on this occasion. If the event has any importance for us in this matter, it tends to point in the opposite direction to that indicated by Doumergue; for why, if a Protestant, should he countenance the girl's vows at all? We shall be on safest ground if, with Lang,[3] we simply say that Calvin was already converted in the October of 1533 and that we know and can know no more than that.

Hunt, however, seeks to convince us that Calvin was not converted until the spring of 1534.[4] His main evidence for this suggestion is that Calvin did not surrender until 4th May of that year his share in the Chapel of Gésine and the cure of Pont-l'Évêque, which had in large measure helped him to pay for his education, and that in later years he called by the disparaging title of Nicodemites those who, having seen the truth, refuse to confess it, denying that he has ever set them an example.[5] Hunt discounts the part played by Calvin in the Cop affair by suggesting that at the time of it he was ready to defend the sacramental structure of the Catholic Church while attacking the saving merit of works. But Hunt admits that this was not a very logical position

[1] X, Part b, p. 27. [2] op. cit., I, 198, 199.
[3] August Lang, *Johannes Calvin* (*Ein Lebensbild zu seinem 400. Geburtstag*, Leipzig, 1909), p. 20.
[4] R. N. C. Hunt, *Calvin* (1933,) pp. 44–7. [5] XII, 65.

G

to maintain, and it is unlikely that Calvin's severely logical mind maintained it for any length of time, especially as he had been reading, without doubt, for some time those writings of Luther in which the connexion between the Catholic Church's reliance on works and its sacramental doctrine was frequently pointed out. In the matter of the benefices which Calvin did not, on our view, resign until some months after his conversion, it may safely be said that consciences on a point of this kind were not, in that age, so sensitive as we think they should have been, especially as such 'scholarships' were not necessarily thought of as being much more closely connected with the Church than those scholarships are today which are offered by colleges with a religious foundation. Moreover, it is quite reasonable to suppose that Calvin for a time did not recognize the necessity of a final break with the Church, even though he had largely abandoned some of its principal doctrines.

We have Calvin's own brief account of his conversion, in his *Commentary on the Psalms* published in 1557, and very little that Beza, or any other of his biographers, has to say adds anything to it. It runs as follows: 'My father had destined me for theology when I was still a small boy. But when he saw that legal knowledge everywhere enriched those who cultivated it, he was induced by this hope suddenly to change his intentions. Thus it was brought about that I was recalled from the study of philosophy to the learning of law; but although in obedience to my father I tried to give it my faithful attention, God guided my course by the secret bridle of his providence in another direction. And, firstly, when I was too obstinately addicted to papistical superstitions to be easily extricated from such a depth of mud, he reduced me by a sudden conversion to docility.[1] Therefore, having obtained some taste of the true piety, I became so enthusiastically anxious to advance in it that, although I did not give up my other studies, I followed them with less zeal.'[2] We should add to, and compare with, this account an instructive passage from Calvin's letter to Sadoleto of 1539, in which a layman, clearly adapting to his purpose Calvin's own experiences, states his case at the Day of Judgement. It begins by describing how the speaker was brought up in the Christian faith, but was denied direct access to God's Word, on the ground that examination of the Scriptures was reserved for the few, whom the many

---

[1] *subita conversione ad docilitatem subegit.*

[2] XXXI, 21; also in Kidd, *Documents of the Continental Reformation*, 268.

must obey; the Christian rudiments which he did receive were
not sufficient to bring him to the true worship of God or put him
on the way of salvation. He was told that his own merits would
gain him salvation, but found that this was of no use to a sinner
like himself, and he failed therefore to find inner tranquillity,
becoming terrified of the divine wrath. But, in default of anything
better, he was following the way in which he had been brought
up, when 'an entirely different doctrinal system was raised up,
tending, not to seduce us from Christian allegiance, but to lead
it back to its source and restore it to purity by cleansing it, as it
were, from its dregs. I, offended by its novelty, afforded reluctant
ears to it; and at the beginning, I admit, resisted it strenuously
and vigorously. . . . It was very difficult to induce me to admit
that I had spent all my life in ignorance and error. One thing in
particular kept me from agreeing with them, my reverence for
the Church. But when at last I opened my ears and allowed
myself to be taught, I realized that my fear that the majesty of
the Church would be impaired was unnecessary.' The Reformers
persuaded him, he goes on to say, that they were concerned, not
to destroy the Church, but to correct its faults; and that the Pope
was not set up by the Word of God,[1] but was self-chosen. They
were able, too, to show that the elevation of the Pope to supreme
power had ruined the good order of the Church. At last they
persuaded him of his error and guilt, and because of his misery
and the prospect of eternal death, he gave up his old way of life
with 'tears and groans', and followed the new.[2]

These two passages permit us to say several things about
Calvin's conversion. Firstly, we must, of course, accept his plain
statement that it was sudden; but we are not contradicting him
if we say that it was no doubt preceded, as all sudden conversions
whose effect is lasting, and all important decisions taken by intelligent people, seem to be, by a long series of mental questionings
and verbal discussions. This contention is confirmed by the
whole tenor of the passage from the letter to Sadoleto, even if
we have to minimize its autobiographical value. Secondly, we
should be wrong in thinking that the conversion was accompanied
or caused by a great emotional upheaval of the kind that modern
revivalism has led us to associate with the term 'conversion'; and
this is true even if we give full weight to the 'tears and groans' of
the letter to Sadoleto. The whole impression given by both

[1] *certe non verbo Dei constitutum.*
[2] V, 411; also (in the main) in Kidd, op. cit., p. 297.

passages is that of the breaking down of the obstinate pride which
in all of us makes it difficult for us to admit that we have been
mistaken on an important issue, by the sheer force of convincing
argument, but a breaking down which was so complete that
Calvin felt compelled to ascribe it to the agency of God. Thirdly,
we are probably justified, although here we must rely on the
letter to Sadoleto, in thinking that the essential change of mind
which Calvin's conversion meant to him was the abandonment
of the idea that salvation could be obtained by means of one's
own works or merits, and the adoption of the idea that it required
surrender to, and trust in, the Grace of God.[1] Fourthly, it meant
also, if we may again trust the letter to Sadoleto, a recognition
that the Papal power was not founded on or set up by the Bible;
but in any case this recognition did not at the time occupy a very
prominent place in his mind. Fifthly, there is perhaps a hint at
the beginning of the passage quoted from the Letter that at the
time in question he believed the Roman Church to accept the
authority of the Scriptures, but held that it misinterpreted them.

Further, a very tentative suggestion may be made that Calvin's
later doctrine of the '*testimonium Spiritus Sancti internum*' was
wholly or partly based on his own experience of the work of the
Spirit at the time of his conversion. If this suggestion were
correct, his exposition of that doctrine would tell us things about his
conversion which we should very much like to know. But it is,
of course, based on mere conjecture and cannot be made the basis
of any argument. In any case, however true it was, it would not
prove that Calvin was yet devoting his mind to the problem of
authority.

And, in general, our investigations up to this point lead us to
conclude that Calvin, even as a result of his conversion, did not
realize that the issue between him and the Roman Church was
even partly concerned with the question of authority, and that
certainly before that time he was wholly unaware of the fact.
But he was already assuming, at least dimly, that the Bible's
authority was high. The exact part which he played in the affair
of Cop's Rectorial Address, taking place, as we think, not so very
long after his conversion, is impossible to determine. It has been
widely supposed by Protestant historians that he actually wrote
the Address, but this supposition is based on very inadequate
evidence. Beza's second *Life of Calvin* (1575) states that he did

---

[1] So Th. Werdermann, *Calvins Lehre von der Kirche in ihrer geschichtlichen Entwicklung*
(Elberfeld, 1909).

write it, and there is a manuscript in Geneva in Calvin's own handwriting containing one-third of the speech. But Beza, in his earlier *Life* (admittedly shorter and probably more quickly written, in 1564), says simply that Calvin had to leave Paris in a hurry because the speech had involved him in trouble, and Colladon, in the fuller and more substantial *Life* which he published in 1565, remarks only that Calvin departed hurriedly because he was a friend of Cop's. And there has been discovered in Strassburg a full text of the speech, entitled 'Speech of some person unknown'. It seems quite likely that Calvin did not write the speech, though he may have had some hand in its composition or played some part in the discussions which no doubt preceded its composition; and that he subsequently made a copy of it, or of part of it, for his own purposes. But we are saved from the necessity of further inquiry into this point by the fact that, even if Calvin wrote every word of it, it would not prove that he was yet concerned about the problem of authority; for it is a treatment of the text, 'Blessed are the poor in spirit', asserts chiefly the uselessness of works for the acquisition of salvation, and does not raise the problem of authority in any form.[1] On the whole, if it was written by Calvin, and if it helps us at all in our present investigation, it tends to show that the problem was not yet in Calvin's mind.

Calvin's first theological treatise was the *Psychopannychia*, according to Calvin's editors in the Brunswick edition both written and published in 1534,[2] but according to Hunt, who has good evidence, written originally in 1534, re-written because of Capito's criticisms in 1535, and not finally published until 1542;[3] a Preface was added to it by Calvin in 1536. Its purpose was to refute the Anabaptistical opinion that souls sleep from death until the Last Judgement. We find in the text of this a scrupulous attempt to prove every statement from the Scriptures, but no hint that he felt himself to be at loggerheads with the Roman Church or, for that matter, with the Anabaptists either, on the question whether the Bible was in itself sufficient to settle the question. The general impression given is that he was now making clearer to himself what was meant by the authority of the Scriptures, but had not definitely formulated to himself its nature, and did not understand that any difference from the Church of Rome on the point made it necessary for him to do so.[4]

---

[1] IX, 873: part of it is in Kidd, op. cit., p. 269 (*b*).
[2] In their Preface to the work in Volume V.
[3] op. cit., pp. 49 sqq.
[4] V, 176 sqq.

But the idea of writing the *Institutes* and of what he would say in them must have been already forming itself in his mind. Perhaps he was in Orleans, where he had written the *Psychopanny-chia*, until the end of 1534; at the beginning of 1535 he was on a journey necessitated by the violent persecution of Protestants which was now breaking out in France. Despite the fact that he reapplied himself diligently to the study of Hebrew, helped Olivetan in the preparation of his translation of the Bible, and, at some time in the course of the year, re-wrote the *Psychopannychia*, he handed to the printer Plattner in August the manuscript of the first edition of the *Institutes*, which duly appeared in print in February or March 1536.

It is quite certain that by the time that he finished writing the first form of the *Institutes* he had fully recognized the problem of authority, and the fact that he was in conflict with the Catholic Church in the matter. For in the course of his treatment of the Church's power he says: 'Has the Church no power? This question makes many of the simpler people anxious, and it is these to whom we particularly write. Our answer is: the Church certainly has power, but power which is given to it for building up, not for destroying; those who use this power aright reckon that they are nothing more than servants of Christ and dispensers of the mysteries of God. To define this power correctly, you must call it the ministry of the Word of God.[1] For it was defined in these terms by Christ when he bade his apostles go and teach all nations whatever he had commanded them. I wish that those who in the past have ruled the Church of God, and those who rule it now, had remembered that the principle of this command was enjoined upon them. . . . Whatever authority and dignity the Scripture gives, either to prophets, or to priests, or to apostles, or to the successors of the apostles, we have stated before that it is given not to the men themselves, but to the ministry which is in their charge; or, to put it more briefly, to the Word of God, into the ministry of which they are called. If we go over all classes in order, we shall find that neither prophets nor priests, apostles nor disciples, were endowed with the power of commanding or teaching anything, or of making any reply to questions except in the name and Word of God.' The passage then treats in order the various classes of people whom he has mentioned, proves his point about each of them by means of liberal quotations from the Bible, and then proceeds (he has just referred to the Incarnation): 'And

[1] *ministerium verbi Dei.*

indeed what ought to be expected or required by man, when the very Word of Life has lived intimately with us in our flesh? Unless, of course, there is some hope that the wisdom of God can be excelled by man. Rather is it fitting that the mouths of all men should be closed, after he has once spoken in whom the Heavenly Father wished all the treasures of wisdom and knowledge to be hidden. . . . What else does this mean than that all the inventions of the human mind, from whatever head they have taken their origin, should be kept away, in order that the pure Word of God may be taught and learned in the Church of the faithful; that the decisions of all men, of whatever rank, should be abolished, in order that the decrees of God alone should be laid down?'

Having thus stated what he holds to be the right position in the matter, he goes on to give what he takes to be the position of his opponents: 'Firstly, they wish our faith to stand and fall by their judgement, so that whatever they have decided in either direction may be determined and fixed for our minds. So that, whatever they have approved ought to be approved by us without any doubting, and whatever they have condemned ought to stand condemned by us. Hence their axioms: it is in the power of the Church to lay down articles of faith and to equate the authority of the Church with the authority of the Sacred Scripture; a man is not a Christian who does not consent with certainty to all their doctrines, positive as well as negative, either with implicit or with explicit faith; and other things of the same kind. . . . Meanwhile, at their own pleasure, despising the Word of God, they hammer out doctrines, in which they later insist that men should have certain faith, and lay down laws, whose observance they make obligatory. . . .' Here follow some quotations to show that even the Apostles had not the power to lay down new articles of faith, and the use of Romans x. 17 ('Faith cometh from hearing and hearing from the Word of Christ') to enforce the following conclusion: 'Plainly, if faith depends on the Word of God alone, relies on it and rests in it alone, what place is left for the word of man? When the power of laying down laws was unknown to the Apostles and was so often taken away from the ministers of the Church by the Word of God, I wonder that they dare to take it to themselves despite the example of the Apostles and the plain prohibition of God.'[1]

Wholly in accord with the spirit and meaning of this passage

[1] I, 205–9; cf. the Prefatory Address to Francis, King of the French, I, 20, 21: 'One of the marks of the Church is the pure preaching of the Word of God.'

are Calvin's words in the Preface added to the *Psychopannychia* in 1536: 'We ought to think that there is one Word of Life: that which comes from the mouth of the Lord; that we ought to open our ears to this alone when it is a question of the doctrine of salvation; that they ought to be closed to all others. His Word, I say, is not new; it is that which was from the beginning, is now, and always shall be. And what a great mistake those people make, who defame the Word of God, which has been allowed to fall into decay through misuse and laziness, with the charge of novelty when it returns to the light of day. . . . Is this to learn Christ, to lend one's ear to any doctrines on earth, even true ones, without the Word of God?'[1]

It is very evident from these passages that Calvin's realization of the problem of authority was no longer dim. From the time when he began to think about religious problems and especially from the time when he began to question the dogmas of Rome—largely, if the letter to Sadoleto can be trusted, on experiential grounds—he turned for the truth of the matters which he was considering to the Bible. But the fact that the study of the Bible brought him to conclusions other than those accepted by the official Church led him gradually to pose the question definitely to himself: Where can I find the truth, and whose statements am I to believe? and to answer it as best he might. His answer we come shortly to consider in detail; as soon as he reached it, he found that it was different from and opposed to the answer given to it by the Catholic Church, and so he found himself ranged against that Church on this ground also, as already on other grounds, principally that of the right method of acquiring salvation. This, then, is the sense in which he recognized the problem of authority, and his recognition of it in this sense is marked by his writings of the years 1535 and 1536.

By the time that the second edition of the *Institutes* was written, in 1539, Calvin had reached a further stage of development in this regard, and one that was final in his thought. He begins this edition by pointing out that all our wisdom consists of two parts, the knowledge of God and the knowledge of man. Then he proceeds to the knowledge of God. God's character is made known, he says, to the human mind by the whole creation without and within us. But man, in base ingratitude, has failed to recognize God in His works; there is a dullness within us, for which we are to blame, which prevents us from doing so. Therefore if man

[1] V, 176.

was truly to know God, further revelation had to be provided. God chose the Jewish race as the instruments of His purpose in the matter, and by this means brought the Scriptures into existence. Thus we are able to see all things clearly, and have been able to do so from the time of the patriarchs onwards. Then he goes on to establish the supreme authority of the Scriptures. Only after he has done this does he feel himself at liberty to proceed to the enunciation of the other doctrines of the Christian faith.[1]

Thus he has not only asked himself the question, Where can I find the truth and whose statements am I to believe? and answered it. He has now understood that it is the question which is prior to all other questions, and that until he has answered it and proved the truth of his answer he cannot logically be allowed to indicate what the truth is. Quite rightly his discussion of this point remains in the same position in all subsequent editions of the *Institutes*. It only remains to add that he was the first of the Reformers to realize explicitly the logical priority of the question with which we are engaged.

II

What was Calvin's answer to the problem of authority? It is a great convenience to investigators of Calvin's theology, as no doubt it was to all those who wished to further the Reforming movement in the sixteenth century according to his principles, that he sets forth all his beliefs in a precise and orderly fashion, so that it is possible to discover in the *Institutes* the exact passage in which his views on any given subject are stated. Moreover, it is rarely possible to charge him with inconsistency either in belief or practice, and it is therefore safe to assume that any view which he expresses in the 1539 edition of the *Institutes* or any later edition will not be contradicted elsewhere in his writings.

Since Calvin is so clear and definite on such matters himself, we have a right to expect it to be possible to find a clear and indisputable statement of his position on the problem of authority, already set down in at least one place in the writings of his numerous investigators. But in practice this is not possible. The same fact is not at all surprising in the case of Luther, in view of the whole character of his mind and experience and the circumstances of his career; there is bound to be great difference of opinion among his investigators. But in Calvin's case it requires

[1] I, 279-93 (Chs. 1-21).

explanation. Bauke has shown that in the history of Calvin-research scholars have on the whole ranged themselves on one side or the other, in the various questions under dispute, according as they have been members of the Lutheran or the Reformed Churches, the Lutheran scholars being most notably represented by Ritschl and Seeberg, and the Reformed by Doumergue and Lang.[1] The general explanation here suggested applies quite well to the special point in Calvin's theology now under discussion. If it is the right account of the situation, there appears to be some ground for the suggestion that an objective statement of Calvin's theology will be produced only by scholars who do not belong to either branch of the Protestant Church on the Continent of Europe, or, probably, to the ranks of its opponents either; but the systematic methods of Calvin afford excellent hope that such a statement will eventually be produced.

In the exposition which here follows of Calvin's doctrine of authority reliance will for the most part be placed on the 1559 edition of the *Institutes*. This is the last Latin edition which received his personal confirmation. On the one hand, it is true that nearly all major issues are settled in his mind as early as the time when he writes his second edition in 1539, and this means that by using the latest edition we do not open ourselves to the charge of neglecting contradictory or changing elements in his thought; on the other hand, the last edition deals with and tries to dispose of all objections to and criticisms of his position which occurred in his lifetime to his opponents or to himself, and gives the final amplification and clarification of his views which they seemed to him to need. No apology is needed for not basing any important conclusions on the French translation of 1560, although it is in fact the latest edition of the *Institutes*. It was dictated by Calvin to his secretaries at a time of bodily weakness, and is agreed to be inferior in every way to the French translation of 1541; it adds nothing to the Latin edition of 1559, and does not help us very much in the interpretation of that work. Sometimes, as Colladon, his secretary, tells us, his words as he dictated were difficult to hear, and large numbers of passages had been previously written out on slips of paper by Calvin and were left for Colladon to insert in the text as best he might. We need only quote the opinion, which cannot be seriously disputed, of the editors of the Brunswick *Calvin*: '. . . the French translation of the *Institutes*, in its definitive and received form, except for the parts

---

[1] H. Bauke, *Die Probleme der Theologie Calvins*, pp. 7, 8.

preserved from the earlier edition, has been edited with a certain carelessness, by hands less skilful and without the guidance of the author. This fact will explain the already-noted difference between the original and the translation. The former is in style a masterpiece of simplicity, elegance, conciseness, and vigour. The same qualities are found only in a feeble degree in the French translation, and only in the chapters treating of popular subjects of religion and morals. Very often, in the others, one has to have recourse to the Latin in order to understand the French phrase, and simply by counting the pages of the two texts it is possible to measure the distance which separates them and appreciate the difference between the concise clarity of the one and the obscure prolixity of the other.'[1]

Unless, therefore, there is any indication to the contrary, it may be taken for granted that all quotations from the *Institutes* hereafter are taken from the 1559 Latin edition.

It is easy enough to set forth in simple terms Calvin's official and explicit view as to the source of religious authority. Religious truth is to be found in the Word of God, and elsewhere only in so far as it is derived from the Word of God; there is no appeal from the Word of God, and no man, nor any body of men, is competent to set aside, add to, or disagree with, the Word of God. God first of all provided the creation as the revelation of Himself; man failed to make use of it, and God provided a further organ of revelation, the Word of God, for us in our fallen state. The Word of God is completely authoritative. Or we may better use Calvin's own words: 'Therefore, although that splendour which is poured on the eyes of all in heaven and on earth sufficiently and more than sufficiently robs the ingratitude of men of all support, yet just as God, in order to involve the whole human race in the same guilt, set before all men without exception His divinity delineated in the creation, so it is necessary for another and better assistance to be added which shall guide us rightly to the Creator of the universe Himself. And so not in vain did He add the light of His Word, that it might become known unto salvation. . . . Just as old men, and those suffering from ophthalmia, and all those who have bad eyesight, if you put before them even the finest book, although they recognize that something is written, can yet scarcely put two words together, but if they are helped by the interposition of spectacles will begin to read distinctly, so the Scripture, gathering together the knowledge of God in our minds

[1] III, Introduction, xxvii.

which is otherwise confused, disperses the darkness and clearly
shows to us the true God. . . . Everything [in the Scriptures] will
point to this conclusion, that God the artificer of the universe is
revealed in the Scriptures, and that what is to be thought about
Him is set forth, lest we should seek in uncertainty some obscure
divinity. . . . We must come, I say, to the Word, where God is
described rightly and in living fashion in His works, while the
works themselves are estimated not by the corruptness of our
judgement, but by the rule of eternal truth. If we turn away from
it, as I have recently said, however strenuous be the speed with
which we press forward, yet, because our course will be outside
the road, we shall never succeed in reaching the goal. . . .'[1] He
then goes on to treat the authority of the Scripture, saying that
if it is agreed to be the Word of God, 'there is no one of such
deplorable boldness, unless he be destitute of common reason and
human nature, who will withhold belief from the speaker. But
since daily oracles are not handed to us from the sky, and the
Scriptures are the only thing in existence by which it has pleased
God to consecrate His truth to eternal memory, the Scriptures
receive full authority among the faithful by no other right than
that they [the faithful] decide that they [the Scriptures] have
flowed down from heaven, as if the very words of God were there
heard'.[2] He goes on to deplore the 'most disastrous error' of those
who hold that 'the Scriptures have no more weight than is granted
them by the approval of the Church', and exclaims: 'as if forsooth
the eternal and inviolable truth of God depended on the judgement of men!'[3]

But this simple statement of the authority of the Word of God
for Calvin requires, of course, some amplification, and will be
found to require some modification. We must begin by asking
what Calvin meant by the 'Word of God'. The passage just
quoted makes use of the terms 'the Word of God' (normally
verbum Dei, but varied when the context allows by *sermo Dei* and
voces Dei) and 'the Scriptures' (*scriptura*) indifferently; and this is

true of all the works of Calvin. It appears, then, that for Calvin
the two terms were synonymous and interchangeable, and there
is nothing to cause us to throw doubt on this. But in what does
the *scriptura* consist?

It is generally agreed that Calvin accepted as Scripture exactly
those books which have been accepted by tradition for centuries
as forming the Canon of the Old and New Testaments, and that

[1] II, 53–5 (*Inst.*, I, cap. vi).   [2] II, 56 (*Inst.*, I, cap. vii).   [3] ibid.

he rejected the books of the Old and New Testament Apocrypha. It has, however, sometimes been urged that he rejected also the Book of Revelation and the Second and Third Epistles of John. The grounds for this theory are that he wrote no commentary on them, and that he speaks of the 'canonical Epistle of John', meaning the First Epistle, as if the other two, which he never quotes, were not canonical. But Warfield shows conclusively that he actually quotes Revelation as Scripture; and that the fact that he did not write a commentary on any given book by no means supports the inference that he did not regard that book as Scripture, since he wrote no commentary on the three 'Books of Solomon', and yet, in conjunction with the other ministers of Geneva, decided that Castellio could not hold the pastoral office because he rejected the Song of Songs.[1] The non-quotation of the Second and Third Epistles of John is a very precarious *argumentum ex silentio* in view of their shortness and lack of doctrinal content; and the chance phrase 'the canonical Epistle of John' is of little significance unless supported by definite evidence that Calvin rejected the other two. Calvin's principles in the appraisement of books which claimed to be canonical were, as Warfield shows, firstly, acceptance or non-acceptance by the historical Church, and secondly, internal conformity with the majesty of the Holy Spirit.[2] It is true that Calvin, on these principles, regarded some books of both Testaments as better established than others, and that he accepted the Epistle of James almost on the ground that he could see no sufficient reason for rejecting it. Yet we seem justified in supposing, in the absence of sound evidence to the contrary, that Calvin's *scriptura* was identical with our Bible. Thus the canonical Scriptures of the Old and New Testaments as we know them constitute the Word of God.

The only question which remains under this head is whether, despite his identification of the Word of God with the Bible, and his ascription of supreme authority to it as such, he actually ascribes more authority to one part than to another, e.g. to the New Testament than to the Old, or than to some part of the Old. If he does this, of course, he contradicts his official theory on the point, since, presumably, if the whole Bible was spoken by God (and Calvin certainly means to say that it was spoken by God when he calls it the Word of God, as we shall see later), then every part of it was spoken by God; and if (as is indeed reasonable) the Word of God has, in its entirety, supreme authority, each

---

[1] B. B. Warfield, *Calvin and Calvinism*, pp. 53–7. [2] ibid.

part of it must also have supreme authority, and there can be no degrees of authority within the whole. Even if we prefer to say that Calvin regarded the Bible as an 'organism'—and there is little reason to suppose that such a way of thinking was familiar, or even known, to Calvin—he would still not be justified in granting supreme authority to the Bible as a whole and then limited authority to some parts of it, unless he is prepared to say also that the limited authority of these parts is limited because they have been taken out of the context of the whole. And it does not appear, from his indiscriminate use of individual texts from all parts of the Bible, that he is so prepared. But although we shall be ascribing inconsistency to him if we show that he granted greater authority to some parts of the Bible than to others, we must still ask whether he did so, because of the (to us) obvious differences and contradictions between the Old and New Testaments, and between parts of the Old Testament; we cannot easily believe that these differences and contradictions were wholly concealed from a man of his intelligence, and we wish to know how he dealt with the problem thus created.

We notice first of all that in the general run of his writings Calvin uses passages from the Old and New Testaments, and from any parts of them which suit his purpose, without any hint that less importance is to be attached to any one than to any other. We can take as an example of this indiscriminate use of passages from the two Testaments one of the passages in which he denounces the habit that the Roman Church has of adding new doctrines to the Christian faith (the passage makes our point the better in that it is frequently repeated in much the same language): 'Does not that law once given to the Church remain eternally?[1] "What I command thee, that shalt thou observe to do: thou shalt add nothing and subtract nothing" (Deuteronomy xii. 32). And elsewhere (Proverbs xxx. 6): "Do not add to the Word of the Lord, and do not withdraw anything from it, lest perchance He refute thee, and thou be found a liar." '[2]

Next we turn to the two chapters in the Second Book of the *Institutes* (Chapters X and XI) in which he explicitly examines the relationship between the two Testaments. He points out at the start that he has been induced to embark on the discussion of the point by the fact that Servetus and several madmen from the sect of the Anabaptists treat the Jewish race as if it were a herd of

---

[1] Presumably because the Church is the New Israel.
[2] II, 879 (*Inst.*, IV, x, 17).

swine, by suggesting that God glutted them on this earth and offered them no hope of immortality. He then states concisely his fundamental view of the relation between the Old and New Testaments: 'The covenant made with all the Fathers is so far from differing from ours in reality and substance that it is altogether one and the same: yet the economy differs.'[1] Having said this, he sets out on a detailed exposition of his theme, undertaking to prove that (a) the hope of immortality was granted to the Jews, (b) this covenant was founded only on God's mercy, and (c) the Jews had Christ as their Mediator and knew Him as such, thus being united to God. The first proposition is established by numerous quotations from the Old Testament, and some from the New, designed to show that patriarchs, prophets, priests, and people in Old Testament times were promised blessings which cannot have been meant to be terminated at death, and were solaced in their hours of trouble and difficulty by the hope of a blessed immortality; the most conclusive passage of all is claimed to be that where Job says: 'I know that my redeemer liveth.' Of Calvin's argument here it is perhaps fair to remark that although in fact the exegesis of Servetus and the Anabaptists is now known to have been more accurate than that of Calvin in its general outlines on this particular point, and although Calvin was especially mistaken in the meaning of 'I know that my redeemer liveth', he here had the support of almost all expositors whether of the Roman or of the Reformed persuasion. He proves his last two propositions at much smaller length, because, as he says, there is much less dispute about them. This closes the chapter on 'the likeness between the Old and New Testaments' (Chapter X).

The next chapter is devoted to 'the difference of one Testament from the other'. It begins by asserting that the differences which exist belong to the category of economy, not to that of substance, and do not in any way affect the vital unity. They are five in number: (a) The Jews were given the hope of immortality under the figure of earthly blessings, but now this inferior method has been superseded;[2] the Jews needed the more elementary method because of their lower stage of development.[3] (b) Truth is exhibited by means of types[4] in the Old Testament, as is clearly

---

[1] *Patrum omnium foedus adeo substantia et re ipsa nihil a nostro differt, ut unum prorsus idemque sit. Administratio tamen variat.*

[2] *omisso inferiori exercitationis modo.*

[3] *(ecclesiae Judaeorum) aetas adhuc puerilis erat.*   [4] *in figuris.*

laid down in the Epistle to the Hebrews, but openly in the New; this also is because the Jews were in a state of tutelage, except for the patriarchs, who were in advance of their time. (c) The Old Testament is the rule of the letter, the New of the Spirit, i.e. the Old lacks the Spirit, the New is engraven on the heart, as Jeremiah points out; the Old Testament is deadly because it involves a curse, the New is the instrument of life; the Old is a shadow and must vanish away, the New will stand for ever. (d) The Old brings forth fear and trembling, except for the promises in it, which, as Augustine rightly says, really belong to the New, while the New brings forth gladness and freedom. (e) The Old Testament confined its revelation to the Jewish nation, the New called Gentiles also to share in its blessings.

Now he has to deal with two objections which have been urged against his view of the matter. Firstly, it had been said that Calvin is suggesting that God is inconstant and changes His plans. Calvin's answer is that he does nothing of the sort, for what he is saying is that God's character and the truth which He proclaims are both constant, but that He adapts the external method of His proclamation to the age which men have reached, and the Jews were children when God wished to reveal His truth to them. Secondly, it had been urged that it would have been easy for God to commit the whole truth at one time to men; why then did He not do it? To this Calvin answers that it is illegitimate for men to impugn the wisdom of God. In any case men require different treatment at different times; God never really took any delight in sacrifices and burnt offerings, but He instituted them for the salvation of men.[1]

To the evidence of this passage we must add that of another in which he is discussing 'external means to salvation' in the Fourth Book. He is combating the view that no State is properly constituted unless it is set up precisely according to the principles dictated to Moses and recorded in the Old Testament for the constitution of the Jewish State. He urges that the 'universal law of God promulgated through Moses'[2] is rightly divided into three parts: the moral, the ceremonial, and the judicial. The last two have nothing to do with morals. The first has to do with morals: it is summarized in the commands to love God and one's neighbour, and it is 'the true and eternal rule of justice, laid upon men of all races and times who wish to order their life according to the

[1] II, 313-40.
[2] universa Dei lex per Mosen promulgata.

will of God'.[1] The ceremonial law was a tutelage for the Jews till Christ came, and the judicial law gave a form of constitution and jurisdiction suited to the requirements of the Jewish nation. Neither of these is applicable to us today.[2]

We have here material quite adequate for the elucidation of Calvin's view on the question whether the Old Testament or any parts of it are inferior in authority to the New Testament. Calvin states and stands by the definite view that the truth revealed in both Testaments is precisely the same; it follows that both Testaments, in his view, have precisely the same authority. The two parts of the Bible mediate their truth to men in two different ways; we are called upon to understand the nature of those two ways, to understand each Testament correctly and submit to the truth which is revealed in different ways in both. It is true that Calvin uses the word 'inferior'[3] to describe the mode of administration employed in the Old Testament, but this seems simply to mean 'adapted to a lower stage of development', and in any case one word must not be allowed to overthrow the general and plain meaning of a whole passage. But although the Old Testament, in all its parts, has an authority equal to that of the New, yet its ceremonial and judicial sections do not apply to us and need not be obeyed by us. This does not mean that their authority is diminished, but only that it is not operative as far as non-Jews are concerned—any more, shall we say, than the instructions given to soldiers in the New Testament apply to civilians. It is presumably on this ground, by the way, that Calvin denied that the Old Testament prohibition of usury applied to the Genevese of the sixteenth century.[4]

This conclusion tallies with that arrived at by Seeberg,[5] Warfield,[6] and Bauke;[7] the last of these points out, following Kropatschek, that Calvin's view is here thoroughly in the medieval tradition, concisely formulated in the sentence from Occam: 'Anyone who says that any part of the Old or New Testament makes a false assertion or is not to be received by Catholics, is to be regarded as a heretic and an obstinate fellow.'[8] Doumergue, however, approving of Bavinck's statement that the Bible is to Calvin an organism of life, argues that as an organism has parts

---

[1] *vera aeternaque justitiae regula, gentium omnium ac temporum hominibus praescripta, qui ad Dei voluntatem vitam suam componere volent.*

[2] II, 1104, 1105 (*Inst.*, IV, xx, 14, 15.)

[3] The Latin word is the same.

[4] XII, 210 (1545).   [5] R. Seeberg, *Lehrbuch der Dogmengeschichte*, IV, 2, p. 564.

[6] op. cit., p. 37.   [7] op. cit., p. 51.   [8] *Dial.*, p. 449.

H

which possess varying importance, so the Bible speaks with greater authority in some places than in others, although all parts contribute to the whole.[1] But even if we accept the contention that Calvin regarded the Bible as an organism, and there is little positive reason to suggest that he did, nothing as to the authority of any part can be argued from this analogy with other organisms. And Doumergue has no passages to quote in support of his view other than those which we have already given and interpreted otherwise.

The Bible has this authority, of course, because it is the Word of God, and this phrase is to be understood quite literally. Calvin nowhere sets out methodically his theory of inspiration; but he says that the historical books of the Old Testament were composed 'at the dictation of the Holy Spirit',[2] and probably implies the same of the other Old Testament books.[3] Of the Apostles he says that they were 'the certain and authentic secretaries of the Holy Spirit'[4] and that their writings must therefore be regarded as 'the oracles of God'.[5,6] Calvin does not tell us anything more about the way in which the secretarial activity of the apostles, prophets, and the rest was carried out, and has nothing to say about the psychology of the matter; but we are forced to conclude, with Seeberg,[7] Bauke,[8] Warfield,[9] and Binns,[10] that Calvin committed himself to a completely verbal and mechanical theory of inspiration.

Doumergue, however, tries to evade this conclusion by pointing out that the French translation of the *Institutes*, or rather, all the French translations from 1545 onwards, translate the phrase given above as 'at the dictation of the Holy Spirit' by words which mean 'the Holy Spirit inspiring and training them thereto' (or perhaps 'drawing them up in array in order thereto'),[11] and the phrase given above as 'the certain and authentic secretaries of the Holy Spirit' whose writings must be regarded 'as the oracles of God', by words which mean 'the sworn notaries public of the Holy Spirit, whose writings are 'authentic'.[12,13] He argues that the French in each case denotes an idea of inspiration which is not

---

[1] op. cit., IV, 70, 71.

[2] *dictante Spiritu Sancto* (cf. Zwingli, I, 260, quoted on p. 76, *supra*).

[3] II, 849 (*Inst.*, IV, viii, 6).   [4] *certi et authentici Spiritus Sancti amanuenses.*

[5] *pro oraculis Dei habendi sunt.*   [6] II, 851, 852 (*Inst.*, IV, viii, 9).

[7] op. cit., p. 613.   [8] op. cit. p. 52.   [9] op. cit., p. 58.

[10] L. E. E. Binns, *The Reformers and the Bible*, p. 21.

[11] '*les inspirant et dressant à cela*' (III, 725).

[12] *les notaires jurez du Sainct Esprit—authentiques.*   [13] III, 729.

verbal, and that it must have represented the meaning which Calvin wished to convey.[1] It is certainly strange that he did not notice that in these two cases, and especially in the former, he had used phrases of distinctly different meaning in the two versions, or, if he did notice this, did not assimilate either one to the other. It seems, on the face of it, that Calvin was satisfied with the French translation and at any rate did not think it necessary to insist on the element of verbal dictation. But it is also permissible to argue from the fact that he retains the word for 'dictate' in his last Latin edition that this is what he really wished to say, and that similarly in the other phrase the 1559 Latin edition conveys his true meaning; but that in 1560 he was not alert enough to indicate that he wanted to change the French translation. But although it may be admitted that 'inspiring and training them thereto' gives a much less verbal theory than 'dictating'—in fact that it, in itself, allows for almost any theory of inspiration—yet it must be maintained that the other change, while it alters the meaning of the phrase, does not alter the theory of inspiration to which the phrase points. For 'notary public' seems to be used in the sense of one who is entrusted by an official magistrate with the task of drawing up a document for official publication, and such persons are presumably required to follow literally the words of the magistrate who instructs them; they are in fact only glorified secretaries, and their writings are authentic inasmuch as their function is to repeat in writing the actual words of the magistrate. In other words, the metaphor is changed (in the Latin, be it noted, it is mixed), but the underlying meaning is not.

So far, then, Doumergue has done little to invalidate the contention that Calvin believed in verbal inspiration. He goes on to point out that Calvin makes several suggestions of textual corruption in the Bible; that he says that the Evangelists do not observe a strict order of time; that he admits that there are differences in different accounts of the same events; that when Matthew erroneously quotes the Old Testament he says that the Greek translators made a mistake and Matthew naturally quoted from a Greek version; that he admits that Jeremiah is erroneously put for Zachariah in one place in Matthew and that Acts in one place does not square with Genesis.[2] This is indeed a formidable array of examples. But we can partially reply by saying (with Warfield)[3] that when he speaks of the Evangelists' lack of chronology his

[1] op. cit., IV, 73, 74.   [2] op. cit., IV, 77, 78.   [3] op. cit., p. 65.

point is that they were not attempting to write chronologically and therefore they are not to be criticized for making chronological errors, and that to say that the text handed down is incorrect is quite a different thing from saying that the original text contained errors. And we may go on to say that Calvin could have used the notion of textual corruption, as it is used by some Fundamentalists to-day, and as Calvin, perhaps, would have used it if he had been pressed by his opponents, to account for all the other discrepancies and mistakes which he admitted in the Bible.

But even if we admit the validity of all Doumergue's arguments, they do very little to diminish the impression which Calvin gives throughout his writings that he regarded the Bible as having come down in every detail from God out of heaven. This is the whole drift of the passage in the Fourth Book of the *Institutes* where he describes the way in which God revealed Himself to man—firstly by speaking inwardly to the hearts of the patriarchs, then by having His message committed to writing through the prophets, the historians, and psalmists, then by sending His Son to be the Word made flesh, and finally by instructing the Apostles to write down the deeds and message of His Son.[1] To quote only one other passage, we may refer again to the words cited on p. 107 and 108, above, where God is thought of as directly speaking through the Scriptures, and the faithful as deciding that the Scriptures flowed down from heaven, listening to them as if God Himself were speaking.[2] And the instances quoted by Doumergue of Calvin's recognition of errors in the Bible are but drops in a bucket of unquestioning reverence for the words of Holy Scripture, and indicate at most that he was very occasionally in a long career untrue to one of his most dearly-cherished ideas.

We proceed to define more closely the scope and nature of that supreme authority which is possessed by the divinely-dictated Scriptures. Firstly, what authority have they for the individual? They are the source, and the only source, of Christian truth; they contain everything that it is necessary to know, and nothing which it is not advantageous to know; the only possible attitude is that of uncompromising acceptance and obedience: 'we must take it, in order that true religion may shine upon us, that beginning must be made from the heavenly teaching, and that no one can receive even the smallest taste of right and sound doctrine unless he has become a disciple of the Scriptures. From this arises the beginning of true intelligence, when we reverently embrace what God there

[1] II, 849–51 (*Inst.*, IV, viii, 5–8).   [2] II, 56 (*Inst.*, I, vii).

wishes to testify about Himself. For not only perfect faith, complete in all its parts, but all right knowledge of God, is born from obedience.'[1] Again: 'our wisdom ought to be nothing else than to embrace in gentle docility, and without any exception, whatever is handed down to us in the Sacred Scriptures.'[2] And again: 'the Scriptures are the school of the Holy Spirit, in which nothing is omitted which it is necessary and useful to know, and nothing is taught except what it is of advantage to know.'[3]

We are not told here, or anywhere, that the Bible contains all the truth about everything; there are matters of history, science, and philosophy on which we know, and Calvin would have had to agree, that the Bible is silent. We are presumably entitled on this view to accept the authority of other books and of well-informed people on these matters, or to decide them for ourselves. But to Calvin's mind they are matters of small or no importance; we do not find him, for instance, concerning himself with purely humanistic studies or their results after his conversion, despite his abilities in such things as shown by his edition of the *de Clementia*. Therefore he is not concerned to tell us what we are to do in such questions. All that we need to know is in the Bible, and Calvin probably thought that if we made sure of discovering and understanding all that is there contained, we should not have much time at our disposal for investigating other matters. The University of Geneva, as set up by Calvin, was a theological University; other studies, at best, were useful for training the mind or revealing the errors of non-Christians. But we must remember, on the other hand, that the Bible contains a great deal of information on matters not strictly religious, although we in our time tend to neglect its utterances on such points; and where it does speak, for Calvin it speaks the truth.

It is after proving the supreme authority of the Scriptures, and the necessity for each individual to subject himself utterly thereto, that Calvin sets out to confute those who prefer the private revelations granted to them, as they claim, by the Holy Spirit to the written Word of God. The heading of Calvin's chapter on the subject, the ninth in the First Book, asserts that 'those fanatics, who, relegating the Scriptures to a lower place, have recourse to private revelation, overthrow all the principles of piety'. We must here remark, what we must discuss fully in due course, that Calvin has just shown that the authority of the Scriptures is established by 'the inner witness of the Holy Spirit', and the

[1] II, 54 (*Inst.*, I, vi, 2).   [2] II, 174 (*Inst.*, I, xviii, 4).   [3] II, 681 (*Inst.*, III, xxi, 3).

awkwardness of the position of one who would maintain that the
Holy Spirit's witness confirms the truth of Scripture, but that
those who claim His witness in other respects are necessarily liars,
is very apparent; for the moment suffice it to say that in the
following argument Calvin assumes that the mind of the Spirit is
finally revealed in the Scriptures, and this is the point of view
from which the claims of the Anabaptists—for they are, of course,
the objects of his attack—are throughout regarded by him.

He begins by asking his opponents: 'What spirit is it by whose
inspiration they are carried to such a height of sublimity that they
dare despise the teaching of Scripture as puerile and mean?' He
presumes that their answer will be: 'The Spirit of Christ.' Surely,
he urges, they will have to admit that the Apostles and the early
Christians were enlightened by the same Spirit. He could have
argued from this admission that in this case from their own standpoint they ought to read the apostolic writings. But they could
have replied that the revelations given to the Apostles were not
necessarily profitable to them, the Anabaptists, 1,500 years later.
So he prefers to point out that these Apostles, whom the Anabaptists admit to have been inspired by the same Spirit as that
which inspires them, insisted on the importance of the Scriptures
and the Christian obligation to read and study them. He then
shows that John xvi. 13 teaches that it is the function of the Spirit
to confirm and seal what Christ has taught, not to invent and
reveal new doctrines. But the real focus of his argument is
reached when he goes on to contend that anyone and anything
that suggests that we should adopt a doctrine in conflict with the
Scriptures is necessarily false, and plainly not inspired by the
Spirit. He imagines his opponents as rightly seeing that this
means that so-called revelations must be tested by the Scriptures,
and objecting that this is to subject the Spirit, to whom all things
ought to be subjected, to the Scriptures. But it is no insult to the
Spirit to compare Him with Himself and expect Him to be at all
points consistent with Himself. The Scriptures are in fact the
criterion by which He wishes us to test Him, or rather the utterances that profess to come from Him, lest Satan should creep upon
us in the guise of the Spirit. 'The Spirit is the author of the Scriptures; He cannot be at variance with and unlike Himself. It must
be that He remains eternally what He has once there shown
Himself to be.'[1]

---

[1] *Scripturarum autor est; varius dissimilisque esse non potest. Qualem igitur se illi semel
prodidit, talis perpetuo maneat oportet.*

Finally, he turns the Anabaptist reproach that he is deserting the Spirit for the letter by saying that according to the New Testament the Spirit operates only in those who give their attention to the Scriptures, and emphasizes the close connexion established by God between the Scriptures and the Spirit, suggesting that man ought not to have put asunder what God has joined.[1]

It is true that this argument does not expressly rule out as false such revelations as may be consistent with the Scriptures; Calvin does not touch on these at all, presumably because the Anabaptists never had any such. If he had been asked what we ought to think about such revelations, should they occur, he might have replied that as they are consistent with the Scriptures there is no reason why we should not accept them, so long as they do not come under the ban, implied in this passage,[2] and often expressed,[3] on the addition of new doctrines to the Faith even when consistent with the old; or he might have replied that as they were unnecessary there is no reason to think that the Spirit really granted them. In any case we are fully justified in thinking that Calvin really set his face against all private revelations, although some were perhaps theoretically defensible, and really wished us to regard the Scriptures as the only source of religious truth; all that we have to do is to interpret them, believe them, and apply them. Nothing that comes to us through the medium of our own minds or spirits alone has any authority at all.

Secondly, what is the authority of the Word of God for the Church and its members? Before we can answer this question we must give some account of Calvin's conception of the Church.

It is safe to say that no Christian up to and including the time of Calvin considered for a moment the possibility that Christianity might exist without a Church. The idea of solitary Christianity, except when bound up with notions of the extreme depravity of the body as such, was not yet known; its origin and growth may have been the direct result of some factors in the Reformation, but the Reformation proper knew nothing of it, at least consciously. Therefore we need not ask why Calvin believed in a Church at all. Calvin would have said, perhaps, if we had asked him, that he believed in it because the Word of God clearly stated its existence and necessity, but his real reason was in this case that he had never done anything but assume it.

[1] II, 69–72.
[2] 'It is not the function of the Spirit promised to us to forge a new kind of doctrine', II, 70.
[3] See the passages quoted on pp. 125, 126, *infra*.

He believed that God had destined from eternity one part of the human race to salvation, and the other to damnation. It followed necessarily from this belief that the Church consisted of those of every race and time who had been predestined to salvation. But he also believed that the so-called Church of his time was not co-terminous with the number of the elect alive at the time. It followed from this that the true Church was invisible. There it might have remained had not Calvin believed as firmly as he believed in anything, in this case relying implicitly on the testimony of the Scriptures, that there is fellowship among believers and that the Christian life is nourished only in such fellowship.[1] Hence the Church must also be visible in some sense or other. So he writes: 'The Scriptures speak of the Church in two ways. Sometimes when they speak of the Church they mean the Church as it really is before God, the Church into which none are received but those who are both by the grace of adoption sons of God, and by the sanctification of the Spirit true members of Christ. And in this case it comprehends, not only the saints who dwell on the earth, but all the elect who have existed from the foundation of the world. Often too by the name of the Church is designated the whole body of mankind scattered through the world, who profess to worship one God and Christ, who by baptism are initiated into the faith, by sharing in the Lord's Supper testify to their unity in true doctrine and charity, hold agreement in the Word of the Lord, and preserve for its preaching the ministry instituted by Christ. In this Church there is a very large mixture of hypocrites, who have nothing of Christ but the name and the appearance; many who are ambitious, greedy, jealous, blasphemous, some of impure life, who are tolerated for the time, either because they cannot be convicted by a proper court, or because that severity of discipline does not always flourish which should flourish. As then it is necessary for us to believe in the invisible Church which is seen by the eyes of God alone, we are also enjoined to regard this Church, which is so-called with reference to man, and to cultivate its communion.'[2]

Calvin's fundamental view of the Church is then a synthesis of the element in his thought which led him to believe in the invisible Church, which is the true Church, and the element in his thought which led him to believe in the visible, actual, mixed

---

[1] cf. Seeberg, op. cit., IV, 2, p. 609.
[2] II, 752, 753 (*Inst.*, IV, i, 7).

Church which comprises all professing Christians, and in which Christian fellowship is realized.[1]

We are concerned hereafter with the actual, visible Church. We have seen that in Calvin's view Christian fellowship is a necessary part of the Christian life and that it is realized in the visible Church. The conclusion drawn from this is that membership of the visible Church, even for those who are geographically isolated from other Christians, is necessary for salvation: 'There is no other means of entering life unless she [the Church] conceive us in the womb and give us birth, unless she nourish us at the breast, and watch over us with her protection and guidance, until stripped of mortal flesh we are like the angels. . . . Outside her bosom no forgiveness of sins, no salvation can be hoped for.'[2] We are not, of course, to suppose from this, in view of Calvin's constant emphasis elsewhere and his plain view on the subject in many passages of his writings, that the Church is the dispenser of salvation or that the community is anterior to the experience of the individual. Christ, and Christ alone, is the dispenser of forgiveness, and only because He has dispensed it to many men and women is there a Church at all. But He has chosen to dispense it, and the whole process of growth in the Christian life, through the medium of the Church: 'He has secured the effectual preaching of the Gospel by depositing this treasure within the Church. He has appointed pastors and teachers, by whose lips He might edify His people; He has invested them with authority.'[3]

The Roman Church to Calvin is not even the visible, mixed Church, let alone the true Church; it lacks the marks which we shall see to be necessary to the visible Church, and it is simply not a Church at all.[4] Calvin freely admits that there are some Churches within the Roman Church—Churches profaned by the sacrilegious impiety of the Pope, afflicted by his monstrous tyranny, corrupted and almost destroyed by his evil and pernicious doctrines, but still Churches; for God preserves marvellously the remnant of His people, wretchedly scattered and torn asunder though it is, and there remain in them some of the symbols of the Church whose efficacy neither the craft of the devil nor the depravity of man can destroy.[5] But they lack the true form of the Church,[6] and cannot possibly serve to represent the visible

---

[1] vide, further, J. Bohatec, *Calvins Lehre von Staat und Kirche*, pp. 285 sqq.

[2] II, 749 (*Inst.*, IV, i, 4).   [3] II, 745, 746 (*Inst.*, IV, i, 1).

[4] II, 767–9 (*Inst.*, IV, ii, 1–3).   [5] II, 776 (*Inst.* IV, ii, 12).   [6] ibid.

Church in the world. Therefore the visible Church must be set up by those who have come to see the truth.

Two syntheses of opposing elements form the basic principles of the visible Church as Calvin thought that it ought to be set up, and as he set it up in Geneva. The first synthesis was between the two recurring types of Church organization: the first type manifests itself as an objective institution, providing the means of grace and salvation for its members, but always independent of them, and normally entered by them at a certain stage of development, the second manifests itself as a voluntary association which exists for the sake of its members, and exists only in so far as it has members, who enter it by an act of will and faith as a result of their personal allegiance to Christ, or whoever is the object of their worship. The obvious, and indeed perfect, example of the former type is the Roman Church, or rather the Christian Church of the West after the time of Constantine; the second type occurs in early Church history in the form of the Montanist and Donatist Societies, but comes into permanent and full existence only at the time of the Reformation.

Calvin thinks of the visible Church, on the one hand, as the *societas Christi* spread through all the world, containing many separate companies of Christians, but not identifiable with any one of them; it is ruled from above by God, not from below by its members, for the appointment of its officers is not really in their hands, though He carries out their appointment by the agency of men; the normal method of entry into it is by means of baptism in infancy; and it is present wherever the true marks of the Church, the preaching of the Word, and the due administration of the sacraments, are to be found. He thinks of it, on the other hand and at the same time, as a company of real believers, who have 'improved' their baptism by voluntary obedience to the Word of God and voluntary submission to its discipline and who take part in the government of the Church by conscious co-operation with the purposes of God and the active ratification of the appointments which He makes. It is well known that historically Calvinist Church government has taken the form either of Presbyterianism, which stresses the former of these two elements, sometimes to the exclusion of the latter, or of Independency, which lays almost sole stress on the latter, though it often retains infant baptism. Calvin himself laid equal stress on both, and exclusive or excessive stress on one is necessarily a degeneration from his principles for which he is not to be held responsible.

This is the view of Doumergue,[1] Werdermann,[2] Bauke,[3] and Bohatec.[4] Rieker and his followers tried to show that for Calvin the visible Church was really an objective institution, and that it came in Calvinistic history to exhibit some of the signs of being a voluntary association because of some inconsistent ideas which Calvin's mind contained, but in definite opposition to his intention. But Calvin insists just as strongly on those of his doctrines which tend in the direction of conceiving the Church as an association as on those which tend to make it into an institution, and unless we charge Calvin with a curious and unexpected inconsistency on a point to which he directed a very great deal of his thought and attention, we must accept the view already propounded. Bauke's book shows clearly that there are many examples in Calvin's thought of what he calls *complexio oppositorum,* and we come to another example now.

The second synthesis of opposing tendencies in Calvin's notion of the visible Church's constitution is of rigid discipline in the control and oversight of all members, and 'charity'. The discipline was accepted freely by all who entered into membership through faith, but was exercised strictly over all members whether after their transgression they continued freely to accept it or not. But the principle of charity demanded that Christians should deal gently and mercifully with the faults of others. The visible Church when it is set up, says Calvin, will not be perfect or consist of perfect people, for we all have to grow in grace; it may even err in non-cardinal points of doctrine. We must do our best to put right what is wrong, but if we fail to do so, we are not to desert the Church, or to disturb its peace by insisting on the rightness of our position in doctrine or in morals.[5] Calvin's attempt to embrace these opposites by giving the pastors and elders disciplinary powers, yet instructing them to use them gently and with mercy, was again a genuine one. But he himself in this case became a party to its breakdown in practice and to the moral rigours of the consistorial system, and is responsible for it in a way in which he is not responsible for Congregationalism in Church government.

Doumergue is again on the right lines in his discussion of this

---

[1] op. cit., V, Part i, Ch. ii, pp. 55–67.

[2] op. cit. (the page cannot be checked at present).

[3] op. cit., pp. 88–94.

[4] op. cit., pp. 346 sqq. He shows that the function of the Church as *Anstalt* is to educate with a view to the building up of the Church as *Gemeinde*; and that the performance of this function is made possible by the growing unity of the *Gemeinde*.

[5] II, 756, 757 (cf. p. 127, *infra*) (*Inst.*, IV, i, 13, 14).

point,[1] for once again he is able to show that Calvin laid great emphasis on both elements in his teaching, and that the charge of inconsistency cannot fairly be made as far as his thought is concerned. We may also follow him when he asserts that Calvin's Church embraced all activities of life, and undertook education, the distribution of alms, the care of the sick, etc., *as a Church*, and that these activities were not in his view appendages to the religious work of the Church.[2] Doumergue goes rather beyond his brief when he asserts that the Church in Lutheranism was merely a cult association which preached the duty of caring for the poor, but made no actual provision as such for this duty to be carried out; but he is right in stating as a significant fact that the Calvinistic Church set up an office to deal with the situation created by poverty. The Church to Calvin was a social organism and a real community, which was concerned with the whole life of all its members.

We are now in a position to describe the relation between the Word of God and the Church in Calvin's system of thought, and the authority which the Word of God exercises over the Church. Because of our ignorance, sloth, and vanity, God decided that external means must be provided for our salvation. One of such external aids to salvation, the principal one, in fact, is the Church.[3] God further decided to carry out this part of his purpose for men by means of the Word of God; and the Church was therefore set up and constituted by the Word of God, through the agency of men, who, in obedience to the Word, took the necessary steps for the Church to come into existence.[4] The Word of God is thus the force which, according to the will and purpose of God, generated the Church; without the Word of God there could have been no Church, and where the Word of God has not been obeyed there is, in fact, no Church, although there may be an organization which goes under that name and has persuaded men for hundreds of years that it is entitled to that name.

The Word of God, of course, continues to be operative when the Church of God, i.e. the visible Church, has been set up among men, for it was one of the intentions of Christ, when He planned the existence of the Church for our salvation, that 'by the lips of pastors and teachers He might edify His people',[5] and it is the

---

[1] op. cit., V, Part i, Ch. i, 41–4. [2] op. cit., V, Part i, Ch. ii, 59–62.
[3] II, 745 (*Inst.*, IV, i, 1.)
[4] *ecclesia Dei verbo formata ac constituta* II, 916 (*Inst.*, IV, xii, 17); cf. Seeberg, op. cit., IV, 2, p. 610, and Troeltsch, op. cit., II, 586.
[5] II, 745 (*Inst.*, IV, i, 1).

'most remarkable of the many endowments with which God has adorned the human race that He deigns to consecrate the mouths and tongues of men to His service, making His own voice to be heard in them'.[1] It follows naturally that the preaching of the Word of God is one of the signs of the genuine presence of the Church: 'wherever we see the Word of God sincerely preached and heard, wherever we see the sacraments administered according to the institution of Christ, there we cannot have any doubt that the Church of God has some existence, since His promise: "where two or three are gathered together in My name, there am I in the midst of them", cannot fail.'[2] In fact, it is fairly certain that in Calvin's thought the preaching of the Word is a much more important mark of the Church than the administration of the Sacraments. He says indeed of the Sacraments that we 'realize from experience that they are more than useful aids to the nourishing and confirming of our faith'.[3] But they are not in the strict sense necessary for salvation, but only 'signs' (*signa*), 'symbols' (*symbola*), and 'proofs' (*documenta*) of our salvation.[4] In other words, they are extremely valuable when we have been granted the forgiveness of our sins and entry into the fellowship of the Church, but it is not necessary for us to partake of them in order to be granted forgiveness and entry into the Church. But the preaching of the Word is, in our sinful and ignorant state, absolutely necessary if we are to have any hope of salvation. Therefore it is, in an important sense, the mark of the Church *par excellence*, although the other mark of the Church is also essential, since the work of the Church is not only the salvation of souls, but the building-up of believers.

The doctrines which the Church through its pastors and doctors preaches and teaches is entirely derived from the Word of God, and they have no power, and the Church as a whole has no power, to alter or add to the teachings contained in it. 'Let this be a rigid axiom, that nothing is to be considered the Word of God to which a place is given in the Church, except what is contained, firstly, in the Law and the Prophets, and, secondly, in the Apostolic writings, and that there is no other method of right teaching

---

[1] II, 750 (*Inst.*, IV, i, 5). [2] II, 753, 754 (*Inst.*, IV, i, 9).

[3] II, 745 (*Inst.*, IV, i, 1). And he sets forth an elaborate Eucharistic doctrine, to which he attaches great importance, in II, 1002–51 (*Inst.*, IV, xvii).

[4] II, 962 (*Inst.*, IV, xv, 1) *et passim:* and the full definition in II, 942 (*Inst.*, IV, xiv, 1): 'an external sign by which the Lord seals on our consciences His promises of goodwill towards us, in order to sustain the weakness of our faith, and we in our turn testify our piety towards Him, both before Himself and before angels as well as men.'

except in accordance with the prescription and norm of that Word.
This we conclude from the following facts: the Apostles were not
permitted anything more than what the prophets previously
had possessed, namely the power to expound the ancient Scriptures, and to show that the things there handed down were fulfilled in Christ; and to do this only at the command of the Lord,
that is, with the Spirit of God guiding them and in a certain
manner dictating the words. For Christ defined their commission in these terms, when He commanded that they should go and
teach, not what they had themselves invented at random, but
what He had Himself enjoined upon them. And nothing could
have been said more plainly than what He says elsewhere
(Matthew xxiii. 8): "but be not ye called Rabbi; for one is your
master, Christ". . . . And because as a result of their immaturity
they were not able to take in what they had heard and learned
from the lips of their Master, the Spirit of truth was promised to
them, by whom they would be directed into the true understanding of all things (John xiv. 26, xvi. 13). . . . Therefore Peter, very
well taught by his Master how much he was permitted to do,
regards nothing more as being left to him or to others, than to
dispense the teaching transmitted by God (1 Peter iv. 11).'[1] This
is only the full statement of what he is always urging in favour of
the Reformed Church and against the Roman Church; in fact,
the main burden of his charges against the latter is that it contravenes the principles laid down above, by not teaching the
Scriptural doctrines and by adding doctrines of its own.[2]

We are to enter the Church and take part in its life, and we are
to obey its teaching; but all the power and authority which it
possesses is wholly derivative. 'Whatever authority and dignity
the Spirit in the Scriptures gives to priests, prophets, apostles, or
the successors of apostles, he gives it in its entirety, properly
speaking, not to the men themselves, but to the ministry committed to them; or, to speak more plainly, to the Word of God,
the ministry of which is entrusted to them. If we go through all
of these classes in order, we shall not discover that they are endowed with any authority to teach or answer questions, except in
the name and Word of God.'[3] The whole spiritual authority of
the Church, and it has no other,[4] is, in other words, derived
from the Word of God and has no other independent validity

[1] II, 850, 851 (*Inst.*, IV, viii, 8, 9).

[2] *vide* II, 852 sqq. in particular (*Inst.*, IV, viii, 10 sqq.).

[3] II, 847 (*Inst.*, IV, viii, 2).   [4] II, 846 (*Inst.*, IV, viii, 1).

whatsoever. Calvin, it is true, acknowledges that from time to time there may be differences of opinion regarding the interpretation of Scripture, and that in this case a council of bishops is quite a good means of resolving the difference,[1] but this is in no sense a concession to the abhorred principle of the Church's independent authority.

The Word of God not only generates the Church and gives it both the total content of its teaching and all the authority which it possesses; it also determines its ceremonies and organization. The basic principle to be observed in matters of public worship is that rites and ceremonies must be founded on the authority of God and taken from the Scriptures. But the Scriptures, says Calvin, do not prescribe by any means every detail in the matter, for they have great regard for human liberty; they give only what is necessary for salvation in general, and in this particular matter they state the general notion that everything must be done decently and in order, leaving to the Church in every age to work out in detail what the time and place require. The rules thus arrived at must be as few as possible, avoiding superstition and the possibility of strife with other Churches which have different ordinances. Charity must be the real guiding principle in the whole matter. And none of the rules which the Church makes in any age are without exception or binding on all Christians.[2] Thus Christian liberty is maintained.

In accordance with these principles, he criticizes the rites of the Roman Church, not on the ground that they are not prescribed in Scripture, for by his own admission very few rites are prescribed in Scripture, and more are necessary, but chiefly on the ground that the Roman Church makes them obligatory, whereas necessity ought not to be laid on men in points where the Scriptures have left them free.[3] He goes on to deny that they have the divine sanction claimed for them, and asserts that they are impious, pagan, superstitious, Judaistic, in most cases, and where they are not, much impiety and superstition have attached themselves to them.[4] But he returns more than once to the point that by being made obligatory they impose an intolerable burden on men's consciences, whereas Christ has called them into freedom. This emphasis on freedom is worthy of note, for it is not elsewhere conspicuous in the Calvinistic system. It is due in part to the practical necessity of justifying ordinances in the public worship

---

[1] II, 864, 865 (*Inst.*, IV, ix, 13).   [2] II, 889–91 (*Inst.*, IV, x, 30–2).
[3] II, 868 (*Inst.*, IV, x, 1).   [4] II, 867–89 (*Inst.*, IV, x, 1–29).

of the Reformed Churches which were admittedly not prescribed
in Scripture, but it is also in part due to the widespread feeling,
often testified to by all the Reformers, of being weighed down and
oppressed by the rites of the Church which were compulsory and
yet useless. But it in no way detracts from the authority of the
Word of God in determining the proper ceremonies of the Church.
The Word lays down the basic principles, but it has pleased God
to leave men free to choose in matters where their eternal salvation is not directly involved; but this freedom is also bestowed
by the Word of God, which is here, as ever, supreme.

That Calvin believed the Word of God to determine the organization of the visible Church is shown by the fact that all the
instructions which he gives in the matter are immediately justified
from the Word of God, and usually from those parts of the New
Testament which describe the constitution of the Apostolic
Church. Moreover, when he has come to the end of these instructions he says: 'so much for the ordering of the Church's government, as it has been handed down to us from the pure Word of
God, and for the ministries as they were instituted by Christ';
and, as he goes on to speak of the early Church, he praises it in
these words: 'although the bishops of those times brought out
many canons in which they seemed to express more than was
expressed in the sacred writings, yet they ordered all their polity
with such caution according to the one norm of the Word of God
that you can easily see that they had almost nothing in this direction which was alien to the Word of God.'[1] We appear, then, to
be amply justified in holding that Calvin organized his Church
exactly according to the Word of God, and in fact tried to
reconstitute the Apostolic Church.

This is the conclusion reached by most Lutheran scholars, but
it is hotly contested from the Reformed point of view by Werdermann and Doumergue, who say that Calvin set up his Church
according to the general principles of the Bible, but not according
to its detailed instructions. The argument proffered is that
Calvin in the 1536 edition of the *Institutes* says almost nothing of
lay elders, that in the 1539 edition 1 Timothy iv. 14 ('Neglect not
the gift which is in thee, which was given thee by prophecy, with
the laying on of hands of the presbytery') is interpreted of the
ministry rather than of the laity, although the elders had already
in 1539 been set up in Geneva; and that in the 1543 edition he
justifies the institution of elders from Romans xii. 8 ('he that giveth,

[1] II, 788 (*Inst.*, IV, iv, 1). The detailed instructions are on the preceding pages.

let him do it with liberality; he that ruleth, with diligence') and
not from 1 Timothy iv. 14. It is also pointed out that the Consistory was set up in 1541, and its setting up is justified from the
Bible for the first time in the 1543 edition. These facts are held to
show that Calvin was guided by the spirit rather than the letter
of the New Testament, and regarded the latter as laying down
only the general lines of Church government.[1] But they seem to
show rather that some of Calvin's practical measures were determined by the necessity of the moment, and that he afterwards
persuaded himself that they had all along been prescribed by the
Word of God, or, if we may put a more charitable construction on
his proceedings, that he became persuaded of the rightness of a
certain course between two editions of the *Institutes* and at once
put it into effect (although in the latter case he should have justified the lay elders from Scriptures in the 1539 edition). But even
the 'Reformed' view on this matter does not invalidate the assertion that the Word of God determines the government of the
Church.

We have seen in passing that Calvin condemned the Roman
Church on the ground, chiefly, that it did not recognize the sole
and supreme authority of the Word of God;[2] and that he condemned the possessors of 'private revelations' on much the same
ground.[3] We may here turn aside for a moment to discover his
opinion of the other source of truth which, historically at least,
had some claim to be regarded as supremely authoritative—the
General Councils of the Church. He begins his chapter on the
subject by expressing a great respect for Councils and saying that
their decrees support the Protestant case. But he denies that
Councils are identical with the Church, as the Romanists
claimed that they were, and points out that in Old Testament
times and in the time of Christ Councils were very far from being
the Church, if we may judge from the aspersions of the prophets
and the fact that a Council condemned Christ; and even the four
great Councils of the ancient Church left much to be desired, for
there was great dissension and strife at Nicea until the bishops
were quelled by Constantine, and Pope Leo himself charged the
Council of Chalcedon with ambition. But on the whole he ascribes
great honour to the four great Councils, while asserting that later
Councils have most seriously deteriorated.[4] It is easy to see what
Calvin's criterion for the appraisal of Councils is: conformity with

---

[1] Doumergue, op. cit., V, Part I, pp. 38–40, from Werdermann, op. cit., pp. 317, 318.
[2] p. 126, *supra*.   [3] pp. 117–19, *supra*.   [4] II, 858–67 (*Inst.*, IV, ix).

I

the Scriptures. If they confine themselves to the interpretation of
the Scriptures, and truly and honestly do this, they are to be
listened to with respect, although even here, of course, they may
be mistaken, and disagree with one another; if they alter or add to
the doctrines laid down in Scripture their decisions are naturally
false and should be disobeyed and condemned; they have also,
however, the right to make ceremonial rules, so long as they are
in accord with the requirements of decency and order and are not
made obligatory.[1] When Calvin tested the Councils that had actually been held by what he took to be the right criterion, he
concluded that the Council of Jerusalem, and those of Nicea,
Constantinople, Ephesus, and Chalcedon were to be approved,
and nearly all others to be condemned.

We have thus reached the expected result, that Calvin ascribed
no independent authority to Councils at all, but only an authority
derived from the Word of God; in other words, he took the same
view of Councils in the matter of authority as he did of the Church
as a whole. He had no objection to the calling of a Council; in
fact, under certain circumstances he would have welcomed it.
But the Council of Trent, which was sitting for much of the time
during which Calvin was at work in Geneva, clearly meant
nothing at all to him; for, in his view, it was based on entirely
wrong principles.

Thirdly, we ask: What, on Calvin's view, is the relation of the
Word of God to the State, in the sense of the legally constituted
government? Does the Bible exercise authority over it? We must
first discover the nature of the State in Calvin's idea of it. All
power and authority belong ultimately and essentially to God.
In view of the corruption of mankind God has delegated some of
His power to men by directly setting up governments and magistrates, which will be necessary as long as man remains in his im-
perfect state—that is, as long as he remains on earth; they are
'the vicars of God',[2] 'the ministers of the divine justice',[3] their
tribunals are 'the throne of the living God',[4] their mouths 'the
organ of the divine truth'.[5] Their God-given functions are 'to
cherish and protect the outward worship of God, to defend the
sound doctrine of piety and the position of the Church, to adjust
our lives to the society of men, to conform our characters to civil
justice, to reconcile us to one another, to nourish common peace

---

[1] vide especially II, 862 (Inst., IV, ix, 8), and cf. (on ceremonies) II, 881, 882 (Inst.,
IV, x, 19).

[2] II, 1095 (Inst., IV, xx, 6).   [3] ibid.   [4] ibid.   [5] ibid.

and tranquillity'.[1] This divine institution and these divine functions give magistrates a divine vocation, one that is not only 'holy and legitimate in the sight of God, but also most sacred, and one that is by far the most honourable of all vocations in the whole life of mortals'.[2] In the performance of its functions the State has the right and duty to shed the blood of its citizens in punishment, since it is carrying out the judgements of God,[3] and it also has the right and duty to declare and prosecute war against other States for the protection of its citizens, although it will do everything in its power to preserve peace.[4]

It is very clear that Calvin thus ascribes complete independence to the State in virtue of its direct divine institution. And this independence includes independence of the Church; or rather, it implies complete distinctness of province. The Church is concerned with the 'soul, or the inner man', the State 'with the setting up of civil and external justice of morals'.[5] Thus a man lives under two 'regiments'.[6] The State may not interfere with the Church, though it is charged with the task of facilitating and protecting its operations, but the Church must not interfere with the State either.[7]

Here, perhaps, it is necessary to pause. It is well known that in Calvin's Geneva the Church took a much greater part in politics than it has been allowed to do in any ancient or modern State, and as large a part as it took in any medieval State. It appears difficult to reconcile this fact with Calvin's conception of the functions of Church and State. No respectable reconciliation is in fact possible. Calvin's theory was what we have stated it to be. In conformity with it, Calvin himself never sought or obtained any magistracy at Geneva (although he sat on the constitutional commission of 1543); he was not even a citizen until 1559; and he exerted no influence in politics, as far as he knew, except as a private man and not as representative of the Church.[8] He was probably unaware that any breach of his theory had occurred during his lifetime in Geneva. But here he did not see things as they really were. There were factors in the actual situation with

---

[1] II, 1094 (*Inst.*, IV, xx, 2). [2] II, 1096 (*Inst.*, IV, xx, 4).
[3] II, 1100–2 (*Inst.*, IV, xx, 10). [4] II, 1102, 1103 (*Inst.*, IV, xx, 11).
[5] II, 1092 (*Inst.*, IV, xx, 1). [6] *regimina.*

[7] On the relationship between the State and the Church within the same nation, compared by Calvin with that of the two eyes in one body, *vide* J. Bohatec, op. cit., pp. 611–14. See also Seeberg, op. cit., IV, 2, pp. 619 sqq.

[8] cf. K. Holl, *Johannes Calvin* (speech at the Quatercentenary of Calvin's birthday, 10th July 1909), *ad fin.*

which his theory had not reckoned. In the first place, he was himself constantly consulted on all matters which affected the city's welfare and always gave his advice on religious grounds; it was frequently taken, and his influence on politics came more and more to be virtually the interference of the Church through its leading minister. Secondly, his great love for the city of Geneva made him extremely zealous that it should be the model of a Christian city, and so he was the more urgent in his advice when it was asked for, and this intensified the impression of ecclesiastical interference. But the third factor was by far the most important: in Calvin's view, private morals were part of man's inner life and therefore within the scope of the Church; to deal with them and punish breaches of the moral law, he set up the Consistory, which was a Church court imposing spiritual penalties, including excommunication. But everyone in Geneva was a Church member, and the city was virtually identical with the congregation, so that excommunication was tantamount to banishment; and it is impossible to seclude the sphere of morals in such a way that the civil law is not related to them, so that the Consistory necessarily invaded the province of the State on numerous occasions. Thus the Church did not in practice allow the State the independence which Calvin's theory ascribed to it. A struggle naturally ensued, from which the Church emerged victorious over the State, although Calvin thought that it had merely vindicated its own rights, whereas in fact it had virtually disfranchised the State.[1] Thus Reformed Geneva out-medievalized the Middle Ages, and the Church securely held the two swords. But Calvin's theory is not in the least affected,[2] and to it we now return.

It is clear that it is a Biblical theory, based on the thirteenth chapter of the Epistle to the Romans, and supported by various passages in the Old and New Testaments. And Calvin quotes Scripture to prove his case at every point, according to his usual custom. Especially does he use the Biblical arguments to confute the anarchists and pacifists, who both denied in effect that government was necessary for Christians.[3] But he nowhere says of the

---

[1] On this point, cf. A. Lang, op. cit., p. 110 (circa). The position after the burning of Servetus in 1553 is clearly set out by J. Mackinnon, Calvin and the Reformation, pp. 160–72. J. Bohatec, in his Preface to Calvins Lehre von Staat und Kirche (1937), promises a later treatment of the way in which Calvin's theories were put into practice. But this has not yet reached England, if indeed it has been written.

[2] In fact, the Ordinances of 1561 embody it in a particularly explicit manner; vide Mackinnon, op. cit., pp. 169–70.

[3] II, 1096 (Inst., IV, xx, 5) and II, 1103 (Inst., IV, xx, 12).

State what he has emphasized in respect of the Church, that it is
created and formed by the Word of God, but only that it is set up
by God. It seems, then, that Calvin thought of the State as having
a function and authority, within its proper limits, which was derivative not from the Word, but only from God Himself. This
function and authority are described and confirmed by the Word,
but not created by it.

Calvin does not shift from this position when he treats of two
other major aspects of politics—the right form of constitution and
the nature and authority of law. On the former question, he says
that it is useless for private men to speak and argue. For a great
deal depends on circumstances, and even if one looks at the
matter abstractly it is by no means easy to determine the best
constitution. For himself, Calvin says, he has a preference for
aristocracy—an interesting preference, in view of the democratic
strain in his ideas of Church government, but one which he
indulged when sitting on the Constitutional Commission of
1543 in Geneva, if the result of that commission's work may be
used as evidence—and gives several reasons for this. But it has
been 'brought about by the divine providence that different
regions' of the earth's surface 'should be administered under
different constitutions'.[1]

It is evident from this that Calvin regarded each constitution
as having been determined and established by the will and direct
act of God—he says in so many words in the course of the passage
just quoted that God 'set up an aristocracy among the Jews . . .
until such time as He produced in David the archetype of
Christ'. Moreover, he nowhere says that we are to learn the true
form of polity from the Bible, for although he uses the aristocracy,
which he imagined the pre-Davidic Jews as having, as an argument in favour of his personal preference for that form of government, he does not regard the argument as in any way decisive; in
fact, the implication of the passage is that we are not to go to the
Bible for instructions in the matter, but rather to accept the
already existing divine arrangements. It might be thought that
he came to this conclusion because the Bible in various places
approves of various types of polity and therefore consultation of it
on this point would not be particularly fruitful, but in view of
his general position in this regard it is legitimate to treat the
conclusion as genuinely arrived at from Calvin's true premisses.

In his treatment of law, Calvin first of all denies at some length

[1] II, 1098, 1099 (*Inst.*, IV, xx, 8).

the contention that the Mosaic law should be taken as the model of all subsequent legislation; having divided it into the moral law, the ceremonial law, and the judicial law, he says that only the first is universally applicable and that the third gives a juridical system suited to the Jews and intended for them only. Each State has to make its own laws according to the circumstances of its time and place and characters of its people, and it is entitled to make special laws, often of particular severity, in times of emergency; these laws are to be founded on one principle of the moral law—which is written, not only in the books of Moses, but on the consciences of all humanity and is rightly called Natural Law—and that principle is equity (*aequitas*); but otherwise they are to be as different as circumstances demand.[1] He goes on from this point to show that it is quite legitimate for Christians to go to law, so long as they are free from the spirit of litigiousness, despite the apparent prohibition of St. Paul in 1 Corinthians vi. 1 ('Dare any of you, having a matter against his neighbour, go to law before the unrighteous?').[2]

We see that the position here is much the same as it is with forms of constitution; in fact, Calvin himself explicitly equates the two matters,[3] and adds to what he has previously said about constitutions the remark that they must aim at equity.[4] Law must differ from place to place and age to age and country to country as circumstances demand. The Bible does not prescribe the character and content of such laws; in fact, the actual legislation which it does contain is to be disregarded as being of a purely temporary nature. But there is one difference which is worthy of note. Constitutions are of direct divine appointment; laws are made by the government which results from the constitution, and their authority, like that of the taxes which a government may impose, is divine only at the first remove. But this fact does not affect the relation of the law to the Word of God, which is not invoked in the matter at all.

It may be objected that as laws (and, according to Calvin's afterthought, constitutions) are to be expressions of the principle

---

[1] II, 1104–7 (*Inst.*, IV, xx, 14–16). On the relation between 'natural law' and 'positive law', the former the norm and goal of the latter, see J. Bohatec, *Calvin und das Recht*, pp. 97–129. Calvin's view of law is misrepresented by J. E. Neale (*The Age of Catherine de Medici*, p. 21), who says that both the moral injunctions of the Old Testament and the penal code contained in it were declared by Calvin to be a proper part of the law of the State. It is true, of course, that Calvin was not always true in practice to his theory.

[2] II, 1107–10 (*Inst.*, IV, xx, 17–21). [3] II, 1106 (*Inst.*, IV, xx, 16 *ad init.*).
[4] ibid.

of equity, and as the principle of equity is derived from the Word of God, they are after all subordinate to the Bible. But this objection takes no account of the sharp distinction between morals and law in the mind of Calvin, morals being within the province of the Bible and the Church, law within the province of the State. It is quite true that this distinction cannot really be maintained and that the attempt to maintain it had unpleasant results in practice in Geneva; it is also true that Calvin's demand that laws should be based on the moral principle of equity is a virtual, though unconscious, admission that the distinction is untenable. But Calvin did make and maintain the distinction, and we must therefore deny that Calvin subordinated law to the Word of God.

The last aspect of politics with which Calvin deals in the *Institutes* is the question of the subject's obedience to his rulers. This was, of course, a matter of supreme importance to those of the Reformed faith, in view of widespread persecution, actual or imminent, at the time at which Calvin was writing. He discussed it therefore with care and at length. What he has to say follows logically from what he has said about the nature and functions of governments, constitutions, and laws. The authority of rulers is from God; therefore they are to be obeyed; to resist one's ruler is to resist God.[1] It is quite true, he points out, that it is difficult to see in many rulers the representatives of God, but God is using them for His purposes none the less. The ruler has, of course, duties towards us, but they are not our business. We must do our duty, and, if need be, suffer as a consequence. If we feel disposed to rebel because of the sin or incapacity of our rulers, we must resist the temptation; their punishment will be carried out in due course by God Himself, and it is no concern of ours.[2]

So far Calvin seems almost to have overstated the conclusion which follows from the delegation of divine power to human rulers—no doubt in his eagerness to prevent civil strife in as many countries as possible and to clear the Protestants of the charge of stirring up rebellion and internal dissension. But he has two modifications to make. Firstly, he says: 'I am speaking all the time about private persons. For if there are now any magistrates of the people set up to restrain the licence of kings (as, for instance,

[1] Bohatec (*Calvin und das Recht*, pp. 135, 136) shows that Calvin thinks of the relation between a ruler and his subjects as being (*a*) one of contractual obligations, the breach of which is an offence against God as well as man, and (*b*) one in which the ruler, as *pater patriae*, stands as a father to his children, and so represents God.

[2] II, 1110–16 (*Inst.*, IV, xx, 22–31).

the ephors who were opposed to the Spartan kings, or the tribunes of the people who were opposed to the Roman consuls, or the officers of the *demos* who were opposed to the Athenian Senate; and whatever power in present circumstances the three orders have in individual kingdoms when they hold their primary assemblies), so far am I from forbidding their opposition in accordance with their office to the mad licence of kings that, if they connive at the unrestrained aggressions of kings and their outrages against the humble common people, I assert that their deceit amounts to criminal treachery; for they are fraudulently betraying the liberty of the people which God has ordained them to protect.'[1] We are entitled to suppose that the 'opposition' here virtually enjoined on 'magistrates of the people' may take violent forms, and we have therefore here a concession to those who assert the right to rebel which is capable of having important practical consequences. Yet it must be observed that the right of the 'magistrates of the people' to oppose the ruler is derived from their own position as rulers, and therefore set up by God; there is nothing here to limit the duty of subjects to obey.

In the last section of all he makes the second, and larger, modification. 'But in the obedience which we have decided to be due to the commands of our rulers, we must always make this exception—or rather, this must be our primary consideration—that it may not lead us away from our obedience to Him, to whose will the wishes of all kings must be subject, to whose decrees their commands must give way, to whose majesty the emblems of their majesty must submit.'[2] We are to disobey the commands of our rulers when they are against God; and this he interprets by saying that we must 'endure anything rather than turn away from piety'.[3] In other words, as his examples from the Old Testament show, we are to disobey when we are commanded to follow a false religion—and only then.[4] There is no sign, however, that we, as private citizens, are to go farther than passive disobedience; violent action is not open to us.

This whole account of the duties of subjects is, of course, amply established and confirmed throughout by the evidence of Holy Writ, and in a certain sense it is true to say that the subject is to obey his rulers and rebel against his rulers because he is commanded to do so by the Bible. He is thus subject in his political relations to the authority of Scripture. But the principal reason

---

[1] II, 1116 (*Inst.*, IV, xx, 31 *ad fin.*).   [2] II, 1116 (*Inst.*, IV, xx, 32 *ad init.*).
[3] II, 1118 (*Inst.*, IV, xx, 32).   [4] II, 1116–18 (*Inst.*, IV, xx, 32).

why he is so to obey is the fact that the rulers' power comes to them straight from God, whom it is his prime duty in the whole of life to obey, and the principal reason why he is on certain occasions to rebel is the fact that the rulers on these occasions have ceased to be the instruments of God and have set themselves against Him, and consequently obedience to God involves disobedience to the rulers. And there is certainly nothing in the whole account to suggest that the rulers have their power from any source but God, or that they are subordinate to the Word of God. Thus Calvin here, it appears, is strictly consistent with his general view of government.

A charge of inconsistency might, however, be brought against him on one count. A subject is to disobey his rulers when they command anything against God; now only the Bible reveals what is against God. Therefore it seems that the subject disobeys his rulers whenever they issue a command which is contrary to the Bible; and this means that the rulers, despite Calvin's professions to the contrary, are to legislate after all in accordance with the Bible. But the inconsistency dissolves if we remember once again Calvin's distinction between the provinces of Church and State. The State, if it truly conceives its function, cannot possibly issue commands which are against God; if it does issue such commands, it must be that the State has gone beyond its province and intruded on that of the Church and Bible. And the permission on certain occasions to disobey means in fact permission to disobey when the State has exceeded its functions.[1]

Here, perhaps, it is worth while comparing Calvin's view of politics with that of Luther.[2] Both Reformers held that God set up the State directly, and that the State therefore derives its authority from God, and not from the Word. But whereas Luther asserts that the State once set up must govern and make its laws according to the prescriptions of the Word, Calvin says that it does so in its own derived right. Thus Calvin takes a step, wholly alien to the thought of Luther, in the direction of autonomizing the State. He is, of course, nowhere near to saying that the State is autonomous in the sense of being independent of divine law altogether; but he does free it from any subordination to Church or Bible. It is ironical, therefore, that while Luther's Church

---

[1] As, in fact, Calvin says that it did when Darius issued an edict that no prayer was to be made except to the king for thirty days (Daniel vi. 7-9), II, 1117 (*Inst.*, IV, xx, 32).

[2] *vide supra*, pp. 50-53, for Luther's view in full.

became subservient to the State, Calvin's Church aimed at and often achieved domination of the State.

We may now sum up as follows the scope and nature of the Bible's authority according to Calvin: for the individual in religious matters, the Bible is completely authoritative; in political matters he is under its authority to the extent of being commanded authoritatively by it to obey his rulers, but much more he is under the authority of God as mediated to him by his rulers. The Church derives all its authority from the Bible, and the Bible is for it completely authoritative. The State derives its authority immediately from God, and the Bible has no authority over it.

It is clear that we cannot ascribe to Calvin the Biblical totalitarianism which we found in the case of Luther; and the former's partial recognition of the autonomy of the State and of the individual in his political relations puts him beyond the Middle Ages. We have, too, in Calvin the beginnings of the distinction between religious and other kinds of truth, implied by the right of the State to publish its own valid ordinances. Of course, the distinction in Calvin is merely inchoate, since the State's edicts are to him derived from God, but the door has been pushed slightly ajar for the State to enter later with a claim of absolute right to speak in its own sphere, and then for science, art, and the rest to do the same.

A very important part of Calvin's teaching on authority has been deliberately left to the last. It is his answer to the question: How is the Bible attested as the Word of God? From a strictly logical point of view this should have been dealt with long ago, for the issue raised is much more fundamental than anything that we have so far discussed.[1] But no injustice has been done to Calvin. For, firstly, he did not see the fundamental character of the issue: this is shown by the fact that having shown how the Bible is attested as the Word of God he forthwith regards it as having been so attested once and for all and does not thereafter ever go behind the Bible to that which attests it. And, secondly, he thought of it as a quite separate question from the general question of authority, which is solved for him by the supremacy of the Bible, and he deals with it as such. Thus we also are entitled to deal with it separately, in order that we may more clearly see the implications of the question and of Calvin's answer to it.

It should be added, by way of further preface to that which now falls to be said, that, although Calvin did not see what an

[1] As is shown *infra*, p. 146.

important thing he was doing by raising the question, yet great credit is due to him for seeing that the question had to be asked and answered at all. He is the first of the Reformers to do so.

No trace of the matter appears in the 1536 edition of the *Institutes;* but then there is no full treatment of the problem of authority in this edition at all. There is, however, a foreshadowing, as Warfield points out,[1] of what he will say in the matter when he seriously considers it: 'our Lord first teaches us and instructs us by His Word; secondly, confirms us by His Sacraments; and, thirdly, by the light of His Holy Spirit illuminates our understandings and gives entrance into our hearts both to the Word and to the Sacraments, which otherwise would only beat upon our ears and stand before our eyes, without penetrating or operating beneath them'.[2] In the edition of 1539, Calvin's doctrine appears fully grown, and what is added in later editions is only by way of amplification.

The question, then, as Calvin states it in his chapter heading in the 1559 edition is: By what testimony ought the Scripture to be confirmed?[3,4] Or, how shall we be persuaded that the Bible in very truth flowed down from God and is God's authentic voice? Calvin answers this as follows in the first place, having confuted the 'pernicious error' that the Scripture's authority depends on the Church: 'The question is the same as if one were to ask, "How shall we distinguish light from darkness, white from black, sweet from bitter?" for the Scripture offers unasked a sense of its truth no more obscure than white and black things offer of their colour, sweet and bitter things of their taste.'[5] Then he turns aside to confute the Roman interpretation of Augustine's famous remark, that he would never have believed the Gospel, unless the authority of the Church had moved him thereto; this means, he says, not that the Church's authority is higher than that of the Gospel, but that unbelievers can be induced to accept the Gospel only by their reverence for the Church; whereas the faith of believers rests on a very different foundation.[6] Our persuasion, he proceeds, that the prophets rightly claim the inspiration of God, is to be sought in a place far higher than human reason or human judgements, it is to be sought in the hidden testimony of the Spirit.[7] Of course, many excellent proofs could be adduced of the contention that the law and the prophets and the Gospel flowed

---

[1] op. cit., pp. 120, 121.
[2] I, 104 (*Inst.*, I, iv).
[3] II, 56 (*Inst.*, I, vii).
[4] *quo testimonio scripturam oporteat sanciri.*
[5] II, 57 (*Inst.*, I, vii, 2).
[6] II, 57, 58 (*Inst.*, I, vii, 3).
[7] *arcano Spiritus testimonio.*

from God. But 'if we bring to the Bible pure eyes and undamaged sense, the majesty of God will at once meet us, to subdue our presumptuous opposition and force us to obedience'. The arguments of reason in favour of the Bible's divine origin are indeed unanswerable, but the testimony of the Spirit is far superior to them. 'Let it therefore be held as fixed that those who are inwardly taught by the Spirit acquiesce implicitly in Scripture, and that Scripture carries its own evidence along with it,[1] and ought not to be submitted to proofs and arguments; and that it attains the full conviction which it deserves in us through the testimony of the Spirit. For though in its own majesty it has enough to command reverence, nevertheless it then begins truly to touch us when it is sealed in our hearts by the Holy Spirit. Enlightened by His power, we no longer believe on our own judgement or on that of others that the Scriptures are from God; but in a way superior to human judgement we are assured with absolute certainty—as much as if we beheld the divine image visibly stamped upon them—that they came to us by the instrumentality of men from the very mouth of God. We ask not for proofs or probabilities on which our judgement may rely; but we subject our judgement and our intellect to them as to something which is placed beyond the chances of human judgement. We do this, not in the manner in which some are accustomed to fasten on an unknown object which displeases as soon as it is known, but because we have a thorough conviction that we are holding unassailable truth; not like miserable men whose minds are enslaved by superstition, but because we feel a divine energy living and breathing in the Bible—an energy by which we are drawn and animated to obey it, willingly indeed and knowingly, but more vividly and effectually than could be done by human will and knowledge. . . . Such, then, is a conviction which does not ask for reasons; such, a knowledge which accords with the highest reason; a knowledge, that is, in which the mind rests more securely than in any reasons; such, in fine, a conviction which revelation from heaven alone can produce. I say nothing more than what every believer experiences in himself, although my words fall far short of the reality.'[2]

Having thus given what he believes to be the only important attestation to the divine origin of the Scriptures, Calvin proceeds in the next chapter to give the proofs of it which appeal to human reason. Among these are the Bible's meanness of style which yet

---

[1] *Esse* αὐτόπιστον.   [2] II, 59, 60 (*Inst.*, I, vii, 4, 5).

convinces, its antiquity, its miracles, its fulfilled prophecies; and
he admits that the testimony of the Church is not without some
weight in the matter.[1]

Calvin's teaching about the supreme witness to the origin of
the Bible is at once elucidated if we distinguish two strands of
thought in his account of the matter. Firstly, he speaks of the
coercive power which the Bible possesses in and by itself: this idea
appears in the statements that we can as clearly see that the Bible
comes from God as we can distinguish white from black, and that
it carries its own evidence along with it, and in the reference to
the divine energy apparent in it, animating and kindling us to
obedience. Secondly, he speaks of the witness of the Holy Spirit
within us, without whose activity the majesty of the Scriptures
will not really touch us. The Spirit, he says, inwardly teaches us
and gives us a hidden testimony; His power enlightens us, so that
we know with more certainty than human knowledge can ever
produce that the Scriptures are divine, and all proofs and arguments are unnecessary. Seeberg tends to suggest that these two
lines of thought are disparate and unrelated, but lie side by side
in Calvin's thought.[2] It is true that they are not identical and
therefore need to be related, and that Calvin does not relate them.
But we can do the relating for him with some ease, as Warfield
does when he rightly suggests that the Spirit creates the sense in
us by which the coercive power of the Scriptures is apprehended
by us; we need such a sense, just as we need a sense if we are to
distinguish white from black, and the Spirit provides this sense for
us.[3] By this, or some such, marriage of the Bible's coercive power
and the Spirit's inward testimony do we perceive and know the
truth that the Bible's origin is God.

We must briefly investigate the status of the arguments which
Calvin adduces in further attestation of the Bible's claim to be the
Word of God. Of them he says that the believer does not require
them at all, since he has the far superior testimony of the Holy
Spirit. They are indeed so strong that any intelligent person who
really gives them his attention is bound to be convinced by them:
'however much men of learning and the highest powers of judgement may rise up against this view, and however much they may
bring to bear their intellectual powers, unless their obstinacy
reaches the point of abandoned impudence, the confession will
be extorted from them that manifest proofs that God is speaking

[1] II, 61–9 (*Inst.*, I, viii).   [2] op. cit., IV, 2, p. 567.
[3] op. cit., pp. 78, 79.

are seen in Scripture, proofs from which it is plain that its teaching is from above'.[1] Yet unless a man possesses the inner testimony of the Holy Spirit all these arguments remain in suspense,[2]
and 'they act foolishly who wish it to be proved to the unbelieving
that the Scripture is the Word of God'.[3] It is, as Warfield points
out,[4] wrong to gather from this that he regards the proofs as in-
conclusive and unnecessary. His point is rather that they are
conclusive, but useless in dealing with unbelievers; they are useful
to the believer for refuting calumniators and confirming their own
faith, and in this sense not at all unnecessary, since calumniators
ought to be refuted even if they do not agree that they are being
refuted, and the faith of believers ought to be confirmed. But it is
not really certain whether Calvin thinks of unbelievers as convinced by them, but refusing to have the faith which only the inner
testimony of the Holy Spirit can give, or as not even being convinced, despite the conclusiveness of the arguments, because of
the absence of that testimony. Warfield prefers the former alternative,[5] and the passage which tells of the learned men who are
compelled by the arguments to admit that the Scripture comes
from above is in favour of his view. But the passages which speak
of the arguments as remaining in suspense until the Spirit gives
His inner testimony and of the uselessness of trying to prove the
Scripture's origin by arguments are in favour of the other alternative. It seems that Calvin was not really clear in the matter. All
that we can say is that he thought of the arguments as sufficient
to convince the intellect, but not to arouse faith. We do not know
whether he thought that they ever actually convinced anyone.

For the believer it is clear that their usefulness is merely practical, not logical at all, for they do not add to his knowledge or
cause his conviction. It is impossible to follow Warfield in his
ascription to Calvin of the view that once the believer is convinced
by the Spirit's testimony the proofs work in his mind in collabora-
tion with the Holy Spirit to produce sound faith. He admits that
Calvin does not actually propound this doctrine, but claims that
it is implied by such passages as this: 'the proofs are in themselves[6]
not sufficient to produce firm faith in the Scripture, until the
heavenly Father, revealing His own power therein, places its
authority above all controversy.'[7] But this passage, which is the

---

[1] II, 59 (*Inst.*, I, vii, 4).   [2] II, 61 (*Inst.*, I, viii, 1).

[3] II, 69 (*Inst.*, I, viii, 13).   [4] op. cit., pp. 84–7.

[5] op. cit., p. 87.   [6] *per se*, which Warfield translates 'only'.

[7] II, 69 (*Inst.*, I, viii, 13).

one most favourable to his view, will hardly bear the interpretation placed upon it,[1] and the whole impression created by Calvin's other remarks on the subject is that he thought the proofs wholly unable to produce sound faith and unwanted by the believer, and gave them only the rather vague function of confirming his faith.

It has sometimes been supposed[2] that Calvin believed the inner testimony of the Spirit not only to attest the Scripture as divine, but also to determine which books are rightly included in the canon. This view is based on one passage in the *Institutes* and one article in the Confession of La Rochelle (or *Confessio Gallicana*), which was composed under Calvin's direct influence and adopted as its confession of faith by the first Synod of Paris in 1559. The passage in the *Institutes* reads: 'they [*sc.* the Romanists] ask, with great mockery of the Holy Spirit: who shall give us confidence that these [*sc.* the Scriptures] have come from God, who shall assure us that they have reached our time safe and intact, who shall persuade us that one book should be received reverently and another expunged from the number, unless the Church prescribe a certain rule for all these things? Therefore it depends on the decision of the Church both what reverence is due to Scripture and what books should be included in its catalogue.'[3] Calvin dismisses this argument as a mere cavil, and gradually goes on to say that it is the testimony of the Holy Spirit which convinces us that the Bible comes from God. It is therefore argued that he must have meant to imply that the answer to all the questions posed by the Romanists, as well as to the first, is: the testimony of the Holy Spirit. But this is not a necessary inference, and Calvin may be simply piling on the 'cavils' of the Romanists without intending to answer all of them at once. And when we consider that he never says once in all his discussion of the Holy Spirit's testimony that it has the function of deciding which books are canonical, although he very often does say what its function is, and that when he discusses the canonicity of Biblical books he uses historico-critical arguments and never mentions the testimony of the Holy Spirit, we are entitled to maintain that the passage does not contain the inference suggested.[4]

The fourth article of the Confession of La Rochelle runs: 'we

---

[1] If pressed, the passage must imply that, when the heavenly Father has placed the Scripture's authority above controversy, the proofs are sufficient in themselves to produce firm faith—which Calvin certainly did not intend.

[2] e.g. by Köstlin, Pannier, Cramer, *ap.* Warfield, op. cit., pp. 90, 91.

[3] II, 56 (*Inst.*, I, vii, 1).

[5] cf. Warfield's argument, which reaches the same conclusion (op. cit., pp. 93, 94).

recognize these books to be canonical and the very certain rule
of our faith, not so much by the common accord and consent of
the Church, as by the inward witness and persuasion of the Holy
Spirit, who makes us distinguish them from the other ecclesiastical
books'.[1] This, of course, says what is required for the argument,
but it is not Calvin's own statement of the case, but an expansion
by the Synod of Paris of what he had suggested: 'this doctrine
[that the canonical Scriptures come from God] does not derive its
authority from men, nor from angels, but from God Himself; we
believe, too, that He Himself gives the certitude of it to His elect,
and seals it in their hearts by His Spirit'[2]—which is not quite the
same thing.[3]

No doubt Calvin's own line of argument is here not particularly
well worked out. For if the Holy Spirit testifies to us that such and
such books are divine in origin, He presumably also fails to testify
this about all other books; which means that in practice His
testimony fixes the canon for us. But Calvin did not follow this
line of argument, though the Synod of Paris may have done so.

Calvin, then, did not think of the Holy Spirit's inner testimony
as fixing the canon. And in the absence of any statement that it
had any function other than that of attesting the divine origin of
the Scriptures, we can assert that it was limited in Calvin's mind
to that function.[4]

We have already pointed out the *prima facie* inconsistency of
supposing that the Holy Spirit infallibly accredits the divine
origin of the Holy Scriptures to the believer, and at the same time
rejecting, as Calvin does, all private revelations purporting to
come from the Holy Spirit.[5] He seems first of all to prove the
validity of the Scripture by a revelation from the Holy Spirit, and
then to test the revelations of the Holy Spirit by means of the
Scripture. Calvin himself is aware that the charge of inconsistency
may be levelled against him, and attempts to answer it as follows:
'The Lord has joined together the certainty of His Word and His
Spirit by a mutual bond, in order that the solid religion of the

---

[1] *ap.* Warfield, op. cit., pp. 94, 95 (also in Kidd, *Documents of the Continental
Reformation*, 328).

[2] IX, 741 (given in Warfield, op. cit., p. 95).

[3] So Warfield, ibid.

[4] A. Richardson (*Preface to Bible Study*, p. 19), having said that when a Christian
reads the Bible in the spirit of prayer, 'God Himself will interpret His Word in his
heart', adds that this is 'what the Reformers meant by the *Testimonium Spiritus Sancti*'.
But Calvin does not ascribe any interpretative function to the Holy Spirit's inner
testimony.

[5] p. 118, *supra.*

Word may dwell in our souls, when the Spirit shines forth which causes us to contemplate there the face of God, that we in our turn may embrace the Spirit in no fear of hallucination, when we recognize Him in His image, that is in the Word. So it is. God did not set the Word in the midst to make a sudden show, for it to be abolished immediately by the advent of His Spirit, but He sent down the same Spirit by whose power He had bestowed the Word, in order that He should complete His work by His effective confirmation of the Word.'[1] Calvin's point seems here to be that God gives us by His Spirit a conviction that the teaching of Scripture is homogeneous with the truth of the Spirit, and thereafter we know that the Spirit and the Word say the same thing— so that 'the certainty of the Word and the Spirit are joined together by a mutual bond', and 'the Word is not abolished by the advent of the Spirit'. He now feels himself justified, as Seeberg suggests,[2] in saying that anything which claims to come from the Spirit can only have value in so far as it is homogeneous with the Word. Or we can defend him slightly differently by saying that in Calvin's view the Bible is something which is once and for all attested by the Holy Spirit, and cannot therefore ever be questioned; the Anabaptists have come along later with revelations admittedly obtained apart from and after the Bible. Therefore they are rightly required to submit their revelations to the criterion of the already attested Scripture. And we can add a further defence by recalling the fact, which we have just established,[3] that Calvin limited the operation of the Spirit's inner witness to the attestation of Scripture, and by suggesting that he is thus entitled to say that any other alleged operation of the Spirit as a witness to truth is ruled out.

But although Calvin's position can be defended by arguments with a fair show of plausibility, we are left with the uncomfortable feeling that it is arbitrary and dogmatic. For it depends on the assertion that the Holy Spirit has attested the Scriptures, and perhaps on the further assertion that He never will attest anything else. The latter assertion cannot be established in any conceivable way, except on the basis of the former combined with a statement in Scripture that the Holy Spirit will never attest any further truth—and there is no such statement in Scripture. The former assertion must be based on the subjective (not, of course, necessarily *merely* subjective) experience of believers. And if the

---

[1] II, 71 (*Inst.*, I, ix, 3). [2] op. cit., IV, 2, p. 570.
[3] On pp. 143, 144, *supra*.

K

Anabaptists claim (as, in effect, they did), on the basis of their own subjective experience, that the Holy Spirit has attested their revelations as coming from God, complete deadlock is reached.

We must finally ask how far Calvin's doctrine of the supreme authority of the Bible is modified by his doctrine of the coercive power of the Word and the inner testimony of the Holy Spirit. So far as Calvin's views and statements are concerned, the answer is: not at all. For having educed from these two things the solitary proposition: the Bible comes from God, he thereafter regards this proposition as in the fullest sense fundamental, and concerns himself no further with its double source. But how far ought he to have modified it? So long as he was prepared to stand by his view that the Spirit's testimony worked only with the Bible's coercive power, and with it yielded only the one proposition, the only modification to be expected is this: instead of saying simply that the Bible's authority is supreme, he should have said that the supreme authority is the joint activity of the Spirit and the Word, but that the only thing which we learn from this is that the Bible comes from God, and that for all other truth necessary for salvation the Bible alone is the supreme authority. If, on the other hand, he had been prepared to concede the possibility that the Holy Spirit could work either alone or in conjunction with the coercive power of other alleged sources of revelation, far greater modifications could have been expected. For he would thus have virtually made the inward working of the Holy Spirit the supreme authority, and the Bible, although it would have still have had to be accepted as verbally true on the attestation of the Holy Spirit, would be possessed of a merely derivative authority. Thus the modification required would really amount to a complete transformation of his view into something trembling on the verge of subjectivism.

To such a thing the whole cast of Calvin's intellect and the whole trend of his religious experience were mortally opposed, and it is not surprising that, having propounded to his great credit the doctrine of the inner, testimony of the Holy Spirit, he circumscribed it as narrowly as possible, lest he should find himself where he did not want to be—at the cost of a very arbitrary attitude to the Anabaptists. Thus Calvin's doctrine of authority remains essentially one of the absolute, objective supremacy of the Word of God, spoken directly from heaven and in all respects identical with the canonical Scriptures of the Old and New Testaments.

III

Will Calvin's answer to the problem of authority hold? He
certainly shares with both Luther and Zwingli the credit of
having attempted to make the content of religious faith objective,
and, as he also believes the Bible to be the repository of all religious truth, it is plain that many of the objections which have
been lodged against their views may be lodged against his also.

We had to urge against Luther that he vitiated his attempt at
objectivization by using his own personal experience of justification by faith to distinguish between the Word of God and books of
the Bible which were not part of the Word of God. Calvin is free
from this defect. Like Zwingli, he held that the Word of God was
identical with the Scriptures of the Old and New Testaments, a
definite body of writings whose limits were fixed long before the
time of Calvin himself. But also, like Zwingli, he is open to the
charge that to assert the authority of the Bible is to assert the prior
and superior authority of the Church, which fixed the canon—
the Church being here properly defined as the personal and corporate experience of Christians since the foundation of the
Christian religion.[1]

Calvin's answer to this objection is different from Zwingli's,
although not inconsistent with it as we have tried to re-state it. It
is that the union of the coercive power of the Word of God with the
inner testimony of the Holy Spirit gives the conviction that the
Bible is the direct utterance of God, and that this is the experience
of every believer. We shall try to estimate later on the value which
belongs to the notion in general that truth is accredited by the
union of its own coerciveness with the inner working of the Spirit.
But we must say in respect of this particular application of the
general notion, that it was untrue in Calvin's time, and is still
more untrue today, that every believer is convinced that the
Bible is the veritable Word of God in the manner described by
Calvin. Calvin might retort that those who do not have this experience are not true believers. But how are we to know who are
true believers? The inward testimony of the Holy Spirit will not
tell us that, nor will the Bible. And to say that the criterion of a
true believer is the possession of the inner testimony is to beg the
question.

A much better reply for him to make to the original objection
would be that the judgement of the Church that the Bible is the

[1] cf. pp. 90, 91, *supra*.

Word of God was only passed because the believers who made up the Church had been convinced of this proposition by the inner testimony of the Spirit, working with the coercive power of the Word; and that this testimony is therefore anterior and superior to the decision of the Church. This meets the objection—but at the cost of making out the testimony and the coerciveness of truth to be more authoritative than the Bible, and, in fact, to be finally authoritative. To the discussion of this point, we have promised to return.

We objected to the view that the Bible is the final and authoritative source of truth, in the case of both Luther and Zwingli, on the ground that the Bible in its original form—if, indeed, that form can be regained—requires for the ordinary person both translation and exegesis, and for the scholar at least exegesis; and that therefore any individual has either to say that the Word of God is unattainable or to accept one interpretation of it rather than any other—which is, of course, very subjective. Calvin's view is open to objection on precisely the same grounds.

Nor can we absolve him from the first of the charges levelled against Luther and Zwingli from the modern point of view—that it is impossible to believe that God imparted the full sum of knowledge to a certain body of men many centuries ago, and has revealed no truth since. By excluding political truth from the Bible, Calvin makes his view slightly less objectionable, but only slightly. We must believe, as we have said before, that all truth is progressively revealed.

By way of a second modern objection to Luther and Zwingli, we said that the notion of a purely external authority was unacceptable, although we conceded that for Luther personally, as opposed to his followers, the authority of the Bible was not purely external, since he knew his Bible before he accepted it, and remained in living contact with it throughout his life. Calvin is freed from the main burden of this charge by his assertion that every believer—not only Calvin himself, or the ministers—accepts the Bible as authoritative because he is personally convinced by the Bible's coerciveness and the testimony of the Holy Spirit. Thus the Bible is firstly internal in its working upon him, and only secondly external, and even if after the initial act of belief the follower of Calvin regards the Bible as something external— as he may well do, and as Calvin himself often does—the internal element is never entirely lost.

This 'internal element' is the most fruitful of all Calvin's ideas

on the question of authority. Few people nowadays are internally
convinced that the whole Bible is the Word of God, and therefore the idea in the narrow form in which Calvin enunciated it
must be discounted. But if we liberate it from the limits which
he imposed on it, and say that the source of authority in general
is the coerciveness of truth and the inner testimony of the Holy
Spirit working together, we have a view which is worthy of very
serious consideration.

It has sometimes been maintained that all truth when it is completely understood and dispassionately considered invariably
commands belief, and that therefore that is true which when it is
fully understood and dispassionately considered commands acceptance; that all truth, in fact, is of the same kind as geometrical
truth. We cannot deny that truth is often coercive in this way;
but we have to admit that what is coercive sometimes turns out
to be false. It is surely difficult to maintain, as we have to do if
we want to meet this objection successfully, that no one is ever
genuinely mistaken, i.e. that when we have embraced a proposition because it is coercive which turns out to be false, we have
really either failed to understand it fully or have not been dis-
passionate. Thus coerciveness as the sole criterion will not do.

Some would say that the testimony of the Holy Spirit alone is
an infallible seat of authority and an adequate criterion of truth;
those who are taught by the Spirit need no human knowledge.
It is indisputable, on the Christian interpretation of the universe,
that the Holy Spirit does in fact communicate the truth, in some
way, to individuals and communities; there are too many unan-
imous witnesses in all ages of the Christian Church who assert
that their wisdom and knowledge does not come from themselves
or any human source alone, for this to be denied; and the belief
in the testimony of the Holy Spirit is congruous with the basic
Christian belief in God as self-revealing.

Now, we may take it that the Holy Spirit can communicate
nothing to any man without his consent. But apart from this
common ground there are three possible views of the Holy
Spirit's mode of action. We may suppose that He speaks through
the human intellect and imagination; or we may suppose that He
acts quite independently of all human capacities and faculties;
or we may suppose that He sometimes acts in one way and sometimes in the other. The first and third views are more likely than
the second, in view of God's preference for working in human
life through human beings rather than apart from them, His

respect for our freedom, and our very possession of powers of imagination and intellect, which are only at their best if they collaborate with the Holy Spirit. On the first view it follows that the Holy Spirit's communications to us will be adapted to the stage of intellectual and imaginative development which we have reached; and this means that no communication of His (until we are perfect) will be inerrant, or at least complete. On the third view this follows for many of His communications. Thus on these two views of the Spirit's working His testimony is not completely infallible. On the second view, His testimony is indeed infallible; but, since presumably our intellect and imagination are not meant to 'fust in us unused', and since many contributions to truth have been made by the intellect and imagination of men, we are bound to conclude that there are other avenues of knowledge beside the testimony of the Spirit, and the testimony of the Spirit is therefore by itself not adequate as a source of truth.

We have so far presumed that the testimony of the Spirit is always recognized as such by those who receive it and that imitations of it are recognized as such by those who receive them (sometimes, no doubt, the same persons). But this is notoriously not so. In the course of history the Holy Spirit has been credited with many pronouncements which can scarcely be accepted now as His, unless He is liable to contradict Himself or the teaching of Christ; and not all those who have received what are plainly the intimations of the Spirit have, despite the utmost sincerity, accepted them as such. Error in this matter is easily understandable on all of the three views of the Spirit's mode of working, in view of the weakness of the human mind and imagination and the strength of human passions, but this fact requires us to see that even if we were to accept the principle that the testimony of the Holy Spirit is wholly authoritative, this principle would have to remain to a certain extent abstract and useless because of the difficulty of applying it with accuracy.

It is clear, therefore, that Calvin has made a very valuable contribution to our thought on this matter by combining the coerciveness of truth with the inner testimony of the Holy Spirit.[1] In the first place, the possibility of error of the kind just described is greatly reduced, because of the check on what is coercive but not true, and on spurious revelations thought to be from the Spirit. In the second place, it must be conceded that if we take the view

---

[1] Of course, we are here separating into two distinct 'notes' of truth two things which Calvin himself more or less identified with one another.

that the Spirit speaks to man quite independently of human faculties, the criterion of coerciveness is unnecessary, and in any case does not help us to deal with the difficulty on that view created by the other, 'non-spiritual' sorts of knowledge; but if we suppose that the Spirit always or sometimes uses the medium of the human mind and imagination, we have at last met a suggestion on authority which gives due place to the three elements in all knowing[1]—the human knower, the object known, and the divine Spirit who alone makes knowledge possible.

The importance of the suggestion cannot be overestimated. If theologians and philosophers alike had followed this cue, we might have been saved from the intellectualism which typifies the philosophical approach to the question of knowledge, from the dogmatism which typifies one kind of theological approach, and from the subjectivism which typifies another.

Three big questions—not necessarily difficulties—remain. Firstly, what makes the object known coercive, e.g. what are the necessary internal relations? Secondly, what is the status of scientific, artistic, and other not obviously spiritual forms of knowledge? Can they, for instance, be regarded as part of the Spirit's activity, although their possessor may be unaware of His presence or even sceptical of His existence? Thirdly, can we believe in corporate knowledge, possessed, e.g., by the Church or part of it, and, if so, what is its character and what are the conditions of its presence? These questions must for the time being be left.

But, finally, something must be said of Calvin's separation of the sphere of the divinely ordained State from the sphere of the Bible and the Church. There are two powerful arguments in favour of this separation. Firstly, it must be urged that government should be in the hands of those specially qualified and trained for the purpose, and not in the hands of the clergy or men acting under clerical supervision, as would be the case if the Bible were recognized as supreme in politics. Plato's charge against Athenian democracy as he knew it was that while people always took their shoes to be mended by someone trained in the art of cobbling, they allowed the government of the State to pass into the hands of anyone, however ignorant of politics, who could get himself appointed, and that they themselves in the *ecclesia* decided important matters with very little knowledge of the issues involved. Similarly, we may say that those who are theologically trained have not as such any special competence for government

---

[1] It is a *suggestion* on authority, not yet an answer to the question put on p. 9, *supra.*

and ought not to be entrusted with it. It is quite likely that the more they know of their own special subject the less they will have had time to learn of the complications of public affairs.

Secondly, the Bible as it stands offers no direct instructions for present-day affairs. It is concerned with types of society which no longer exist, and was written by people who had no knowledge of the questions which confront a modern statesman. Besides, most of the political injunctions, and all those of a detailed nature, to be found in the Bible appear in the Old Testament and are therefore of at least a sub-Christian character—a fact inadequately realized by those Puritans who tried to govern England according to the Scriptures, or by the Dutch settlers in South Africa.

It looks, then, as if the State, since it is, according to Calvin, to reckon itself ordained by God, will do best to consult, not the Church or the Bible about the policies which it is to pursue or the laws which it is to make, but God directly, and to govern according to His Will revealed to it for every separate situation.

But there are also powerful arguments on the other side. Even if the State recognizes itself as divinely ordained, by separating its sphere from that of the Bible we run into grave danger of supposing that politics has nothing to do with religion or morals, and proceeds according to its own laws—revealed, no doubt, directly by God. But, in fact, no political question is purely political, nor any economic question purely economic. Whether, for instance, the profit of individuals should be limited by the State is at least partially, and probably fundamentally, a moral and religious question, and to treat it as if it were not is to rule out the possibility of solving it. And although the Bible contains no specific economic or political instructions which can be advantageously applied to a modern situation without more ado, it does, in the New Testament, contain the moral and religious principles according to which the fundamental issues of government are to be settled.

In any case, the doctrine that God reveals himself to rulers, because they are rulers, independently of the usual media of Bible and Church, has no very satisfactory basis either in theology or experience. At any rate, those rulers who insisted most strongly on their divine right and expected immediate divine guidance on political matters have not always been the wisest statesmen, and the wisest statesmen have often been those who consulted both Church and Bible.

And, thirdly, the States which have recognized themselves, and have been recognized by the Church, as having been divinely ordained, and have on that ground claimed, and been granted by the Church, complete autonomy in their own sphere, show in history a depressing tendency to degenerate into States which claim the same autonomy, and force the Church to grant it, on the ground of their own absolute right, and act in future without regard to any divine laws, real or imagined; religious absolutism becomes secular absolutism. We have noted the irony of history by which the State in Lutheran countries was granted by the Church more autonomy than in Calvinist countries, although Calvin's theory granted it much more than Luther's; and it is in Lutheran countries that the tendency to secular absolutism has been most manifest, Frederick the Great affording by no means the only or the first example of State absolutism there. In England the doctrine of the divine right of kings becomes in the hands of Thomas Hobbes the doctrine of the absolute right of any government which can establish itself; and although Hobbes was not 'respectable', while the Vicar of Bray was teaching his flock,

> Kings are by God appointed;
> And damned are those who dare resist
> Or touch the Lord's anointed,

Charles the Second was ruling England without much obvious consultation of his divine Overlord.

It appears from the above argument that Calvin's sheer separation of the sphere of the State from that of the Bible is not satisfactory; but also that he was right in refusing to subordinate the State to the Bible's detailed instructions. He can help us here to develop a theory according to which the State, acknowledging its divine commission, shall be supreme in the taking of political decisions, in virtue of its knowledge of the technique of government and of the actual situation; and the Church, itself autonomous under God, shall publicly enunciate, as the interpreter of the Biblical message to each generation, the moral and religious principles on which the common life of men ought to be founded.

CONCLUSION

WE embarked on this inquiry with the reasonable hope that Luther or Zwingli or Calvin would solve for us the problem of authority. That hope has been disappointed, and the problem is still unsolved. The basic reason for the failure of the three great Reformers to do what we expected of them, if we set aside the question of their intellectual and spiritual capacity and the immense amount of practical work which in each case left them little time for constructive thinking, is this: not one of them was able to free himself entirely—Calvin most of the three, but not even he entirely—from the medieval error that the source of authority is necessarily to be found in some place wholly outside the individual. While this error prevails, the problem is insoluble.

But we have learned from Luther that there is a Word of God, a revealed truth about the universe, if we can only find it. From Calvin we have picked up the hint that true knowledge comes from the interaction of the knower, the known, and the Spirit of God; and he has also told us something of the nature and limitations of the State's authority. And the attempts of all of them to locate the seat of authority have enabled us to clear the ground of many untenable views which have nevertheless affected the lives of men and societies. So, perhaps, the inquiry has not been entirely useless.

BIBLIOGRAPHY

J. W. ALLEN. '*Martin Luther*' in *The Social and Political Ideas of Some Great Thinkers of the Renaissance and Reformation*, edited by F. J. C. Hearnshaw. London, 1925.

AUGUSTINE. *Corpus Scriptorum Ecclesiasticorum Latinorum*, Vol. 40. Vienna, 1899–1900.

H. BAUKE. *Die Probleme der Theologie Calvins*. Leipzig, 1922.

K. BIHLMEYER. *Kirchengeschichte.*

L. E. E. BINNS. *The Reformers and the Bible*. Cambridge, 1923.

J. BOHATEC. *Calvin und das Recht*. Feudingen i. Westfalen, 1934.

—— *Calvins Lehre von Staat und Kirche*. Breslau, 1937.

JOHN CALVIN. *Calvini Opera*, Vols. I–LVII, in the *Corpus Reformatorum* (XXIX–LXXXVI). Brunswick, 1863–97. Berlin, 1900.

P. DREWS. *Entsprach das Staatskirchentum dem Ideale Luthers?* in *Zeitschrift für Theologie und Kirche*, 18, 1908.

E. DOUMERGUE. *Jean Calvin*. Lausanne, 1899 onwards.

A. FARNER. *Die Lehre von Kirche und Staat bei Zwingli.*

H. GRISAR. *Luther*. Freiburg i. Breisgau, 1911–12.

T. HARNACK. *Luthers Theologie*. Erlangen, 1862.

W. HEINSIUS. *Martin Luther: Vorreden zur Heiligen Schrift*. Munich, 1934.

H. HERMELINK. *Zu Luthers Gedanken über Idealgemeinden und von weltlicher Obrigkeit* in *Zeitschrift für Kirchengeschichte*, 29, 1908.

F. HOFMANN. *Der Kirchenbegriff des Heiligen Augustinus*. Munich, 1933.

K. HOLL. *Johannes Calvin* (a speech at the Quatercentenary of Calvin's Birthday, 10th July 1909).

—— *Gesammelte Aufsätze zur Kirchengeschichte, I: Luther*. Sixth Edition, Tübingen, 1932.

R. N. C. HUNT. *Calvin*. London, 1933.

J. HUS. *Magistri Johannis Hus Opera Omnia*. Prague, 1903 onwards.

B. J. KIDD. *Documents of the Continental Reformation*. Oxford, 1911.

—— *Documents Illustrative of the History of the Church*. London, 1920 and 1923.

—— *A History of the Church to A.D. 461*. 3 vols. Oxford, 1922.

W. KÖHLER. In *Deutsche Zeitschrift für Kirchenrecht*, 1906.

—— *Zwingli and Luther*, I. Leipzig, 1924.

A. LANG. *Johannes Calvin: Ein Lebensbild zu seinem 400. Geburtstag*. Leipzig, 1909.

T. M. LINDSAY. *History of the Reformation* (2 vols.). Edinburgh, 1906.

MARTIN LUTHER. *Werke.* Weimar, 1883 onward. (Quoted as *W.A.*)

A. C. McGIFFERT. *Protestant Thought before Kant.* London, 1911.

J. MACKINNON. *Luther and the Reformation.* 4 vols. London, 1925–30.

—— *Calvin and the Reformation.* London, 1936.

J. MACMURRAY. *The Clue to History.* London, 1938.

K. MATTHES. *Luther und die Obrigkeit.* Munich, 1937.

MEINECKE. *Luther über christliches Gemeinwesen und christlichen Staat* in *Historische Zeitschrift*, Vol. 121.

NAGEL. *Zwinglis Stellung zur Schrift.*

J. E. NEALE. *The Age of Catherine de Medici.* London, 1943.

W. P. PATERSON. *The Rule of Faith.* London, 1932.

M PIETTE. *John Wesley in the Evolution of Protestantism.* (English translation of *La Réaction wesléyenne dans l'évolution protestante: étude d'histoire religieuse.*) London, 1937.

A. RICHARDSON. *Preface to Bible Study.* London, 1943.

RIEKER. *Die rechtliche Stellung der evangelischen Kirche Deutschlands.* 1903.

A. SABATIER. *Religions of Authority and the Religion of the Spirit.* (English translation of *Les Religions d'autorité et la religion de l'esprit*, Paris, 1904.) London, 1904.

P. SCHEMPP. *Luthers Stellung zur Heiligen Schrift.*

A. SCHULTZE. *Stadtgemeinde und Reformation.* 1903.

R. SEEBERG. *Lehrbuch der Dogmengeschichte.* Leipzig, 1920–33.

P. SMITH. *Life and Letters of Martin Luther.* London, 1911.

R. SOHM. *Kirchenrecht.*

R. H. TAWNEY. *Religion and the Rise of Capitalism.* London, 1926.

E. TROELTSCH. *Protestantism and Progress.* (English translation of *Protestantisches Christentum und Kirche in der Neuzeit.*) London, 1912.

—— *Social Teaching of the Christian Churches.* (English translation of *Die Sociallehre der Christlichen Kirchen und Gruppen.*) London, 1931.

H. WACE. *Principles of the Reformation.* London, 1910.

B. B. WARFIELD. *Calvin and Calvinism.* New York, 1931.

T. WERDERMANN. *Calvins Lehre von der Kirche in ihrer geschichtlichen Entwicklung.* Elberfeld, 1909.

J. WYCLIF. *Wyclif's Latin Works.* 36 vols. London, 1883–1922.

ULRICH ZWINGLI. *Zwinglis Werke.* Vols. I–V, in the *Corpus Reformatorum* (LXXXVIII. sqq.). Berlin, 1905 onwards.

INDEX

Printed in Great Britain by
The Camelot Press Ltd., London and Southampton

DATE DUE

5/28/75			
OCT 2 8 '90			
GAYLORD			PRINTED IN U.S.A.